EATING IN
COLOR

EATING IN COLOR

DELICIOUS, HEALTHY RECIPES FOR YOU AND YOUR FAMILY

FRANCES LARGEMAN-ROTH

PHOTOGRAPHS BY QUENTIN BACON

Stewart, Tabori & Chang | New York

DEDICATION

To Jon, for giving me the freedom to chase my dreams, and for your patience and ever-ready appetite.

To Willa, for inspiring me to write this book, and for asking so many good questions.

To Leo, for trying everything on your plate, and for always being there with a smile.

I love you all.

Published in 2014 by Stewart, Tabori & Chang

An imprint of ABRAMS

Library of Congress Control Number: 2013935968

ISBN: 978-1-61769-029-7

Design: Modern Good, Matthew Bouloutian & Christine Mikus

Production Manager: True Sims

The text of this book was composed in Scout and Ernestine Offc Pro.

Printed and bound in China.

10 9 8 7 6 5 4 3 2 1

Stewart, Tabori & Chang books are available at special discounts when purchased in quantity for premiums and promotions as well as fundraising or educational use. Special editions can also be created to specification. For details, contact specialsales@abramsbooks.com or the address below.

This book is not intended as a substitute for medical advice from a qualified physician. The intent of this book is to provide accurate general information in regard to the subject matter covered. If medical advice or other expert help is needed, the services of an appropriate medical professional should be sought.

ABRAMS
THE ART OF BOOKS SINCE 1949

115 West 18th Street
New York, NY 10011
www.abramsbooks.com

Acknowledgments

If a book is a labor of love, then it can only be as good as the relationships that formed to create it. I am extremely lucky to have so many smart, talented people to draw on for their expertise and friendship.

Huge thanks to my "dream team"—Quentin Bacon, Stephana Bottom, and Philippa Brathwaite. Without them this book would just be a nice, but visually boring assortment of printed words. You understood my vision from day one and worked your tails off (without proper lunch breaks!) to help me achieve it. Quentin—your eye is so well trained that your shots all appear effortless. And who knew you were a baby wrangler! Stephana and Paige, thank you for making my food look so mouthwatering and for helping everyone keep their ducks in a row. Philippa, I loved having my bed covered with plates, cutlery, and glasses from ABC Carpet & Home, Canvas, Ochre, Aero, and Dean & Deluca.

A big *merci beaucoup* to Mary Drennen for her tireless nutritional number crunching.

Thanks to Ray Guh at Christo salon for making me look my very best. And Doug McIntosh at Sahag for making my hair match my daughter's. And to Karen Shapiro for keeping our shirts tucked in and making sure we didn't clash.

Thanks to the following companies for sending their wonderful fresh produce and other products that helped make the recipes come together and kept the crew alert: California figs, Chobani, Driscoll's, Earthbound Farm, Keurig, Madhava Natural Sweeteners, Melissa's Produce, Niman Ranch, Ocean Spray, Peeled Snacks, and TruRoots.

Thank you to my friends and family (especially Ann Sheffield) for believing in me and going to the mat to spread the word about *Eating in Color*.

To Jessica at Dystel & Goderich. Thanks for weathering my false starts and helping me find my voice. Your cheerleading went a long way.

Thanks to the entire Flutie team: Hilary, Robert, Danielle, and the rest of the crew. Your creative guidance, support, encouragement, and BIG picture view helped me see the light at the end of the tunnel.

To all the folks at *Cooking Light*—you have been amazing to work with and I so appreciate your support!

Thanks to Claire Bamundo, publicity director extraordinaire, for getting the word out about this book in just the right way. Everyone else at Stewart, Tabori & Chang—I so appreciate you trusting me enough to create a book that was both nutritious and delicious. To my publicist, Danielle Zaria Praport, thank you for working so hard to get the *Eating in Color* message out!

And finally, thank you to Leslie Stoker, for believing in my vision of creating a book that celebrates both the fun and healthy attributes of all those amazingly colorful foods.

CONTENTS

I was not born a foodie. My love of, respect for, and fascination with food and its health-giving properties are something I had to come around to—or back to.

I grew up in an odd setting. I was born to a German mother and a Jewish, Brooklyn-raised military father, who somehow decided to raise their brood of five children in a small town on a Native American reservation in western New York.

For as long as I can remember, I always had a strong passion for animals and science, and from the age of five, I was hell-bent on becoming a veterinarian. I had little interest in food or cooking, but luckily this didn't deter my mother from teaching me about it from a young age. Mom grew up in the restaurant business in a small spa town in Germany and learned the finer points of hospitality while she was still in diapers. These were skills I wouldn't come to appreciate until college, when I was forced to learn how to cook and shop for the residents of the vegetarian co-op I lived in during my sophomore and junior years at Cornell University. But learn I did, and a nascent interest in food and all that it can do for us became a full-fledged obsession by my fourth year of college, leading me to stay an extra year and switch my major from animal science to human nutrition.

The hippie co-op may have piqued my interest in nutrition, but once I dug into it, I realized, for very personal reasons, I would make it not just a career choice but a life path. My father had type 2 diabetes, high blood pressure, and central adiposity. (The latter is science-speak for excess fat in the belly. I'm sure he would have preferred being called barrel-chested.) He had also loved food, but leaned toward fatty and cured meats, like pastrami and corned beef. And while my mother loved fruits and vegetables, her cooking style involved a fair amount of butter and was not what I'd call "light."

Though Dad had been a dentist and had a general understanding of nutrition, he hadn't ever applied it to his daily life. He didn't manage his diabetes well through diet and he didn't take time out of his busy work and home life for exercise and stress reduction. All of these factors led him to die of a massive heart attack at the age of sixty-two. I was twelve years old.

Later, my classes at Cornell taught me the basics about human nutrition, and the pieces to the puzzle of why I lost my dad came together. I realized that he didn't have to die so young—his multiple health issues were a result of his diet and lifestyle. I wanted to turn the clock back and teach him everything I had learned; ultimately, I put those energies toward teaching other people about how to eat right and live healthy, active lifestyles.

Fruits and vegetables contain compounds that reduce the risk of heart disease and stroke, some cancers, chronic respiratory diseases, diabetes, and obesity, which is why nutrition experts have been trying to get Americans to eat more of them for years. I realize now that what my dad was missing, along with regular exercise, was more of these disease-busting, nutrient-packed foods. Most Americans are extremely challenged when it comes to getting enough fruits and vegetables in their diets. A 2010 report by the Centers for Disease Control and Prevention (CDC) found that only 26 percent of Americans are getting the recommended three servings a day of vegetables. We do slightly better in the fruit department—33 percent of us eat the suggested two servings daily. The majority of messages that aim to entice us to eat more of the good stuff focus on the fiber or phytonutrient content of these healthy foods. I could be wrong, but apart from a few health zealots, it seems most of us are moved by flavor when we make our food choices, and not the latest clinical research. People don't go to the store to buy zeaxanthin or anthocyanins, they go to pick up a few zucchini for dinner and blackberries for tomorrow's breakfast.

Although you'll find detailed information about the ingredients I use in *Eating in Color*—when they're in season, how to choose them, how to store them, and, of course, how to use them—I don't want you to get too hung up on the details. My goal with this cookbook is not to get you to focus on specific nutrients, but just to eat more fruits, vegetables, and whole grains each day. Since hardly any of us are getting enough, there's lots of room for improvement! I hope that this book gets you to look at the contents of your shopping cart a bit more closely and gets you to head back to the produce department for a few more items, take your kids to a farmer's market, join a CSA, or try a tough-to-pronounce whole grain. And I hope that you'll then share that experience of wanting more with others. More color, more flavor, and absolutely more fun.

What Eating in Color Is About

Like most moms of young kids, I have a mad dash each night to put something on the table that my kids will eat. And of course as a dietitian, I want what I'm serving to also be nutritious. But two-year-olds can be picky, and I found myself offering a slate of foods that were bland and colorless: pasta, chicken, cheese, and sometimes corn. Though my husband didn't complain, I was bored with what we were eating, and I knew I had to be proactive about fixing the problem.

It was around the same time that my daughter Willa's daycare class began a "color study." The children didn't just learn to identify colors, they also discovered what happens when different colors are blended together and where to find various colors in nature. She was obsessed with telling us the color of everything, from her crayons to her carrots. Color! That got me thinking . . . now that Willa was excited about colors, I realized I could entice her to expand her palate by offering up reds, oranges, and greens instead of beets, sweet potatoes, and broccoli.

I figured that if I was feeling challenged to add more color to our meals, other families must be having the same struggle. And so we set off on a new, vibrant food adventure. I started thinking about ingredients differently—not only about their health-giving properties, but how they'd add to the brightness of a dish, or how an unfamiliar ingredient could be used in a tried-and-true way. This is how quinoa ended up in a quiche and chia seeds found their way into my panna cotta.

Joining a CSA was an important step in our colorification. After debating its merits (lots of low-cost fresh produce) and drawbacks (another thing to do on the weekends) for a few years, I finally convinced my husband

it was worth it. We started getting our shares of locally grown Long Island vegetables, fruit, eggs, and flowers in early summer and continued all through the fall. Not every haul was amazing: There were mangy looking herbs, aphid-eaten Brussels sprouts, and sun-cooked berries, but for the most part everything was high quality. We made great use of our twice-monthly pickups, and brought a whole world of color into my kitchen and ultimately onto our plates. We got to try lemon cucumbers, red turnips, donut peaches, and Brandywine heirloom tomatoes. And I got to have lots of fun experimenting with it all! The delicious results are within these pages, and I hope you and your family find them to be just as enjoyable as we do.

Naturally, in a book about eating in color, you'll find lots of brightly colored ingredients like fruits and vegetables. But you will also find more subdued, earth-toned ingredients like whole grains, seeds, and even chocolate (happy dance!). There's so much promising research that shows that all of these foods can help make our diets healthier and more nutrient-packed. From a culinary perspective, they also add texture, flavor, and interest. That's why, in addition to the traditional ROYGBIV colors of the spectrum, you will find an entire chapter devoted to Black and Tan foods.

And while I'd estimate that 90 percent of the ingredients in the book are plant-based, this is not a vegetarian cookbook. You'll find seafood, eggs, poultry, lamb, and even bacon in the recipes. Why? Because they're all delicious and I want you to love the dishes! Used judiciously, I believe there's room in our diets for animal protein, cake, cocktails, and other celebratory foods. And if you eat close to the earth 90 percent of the day, my philosophy is that you can be less than perfect the other 10 percent of the time.

If you can incorporate even a few of the recipes in this cookbook into your repertoire each week, you'll be significantly upping the amount of fruits, vegetables, and whole grains you and your family consume. And that means lots of goodies: more fiber, more nutrients, and more antioxidants to improve your long-term health. Consider this book a jumping off point—it should get you thinking about ways that you can add color to your go-to recipes, possibly adding an extra vegetable to a basic salad, or mixing a fresh or dried fruit into a favorite muffin recipe.

My Rules for Eating in Color

This isn't a diet book, but it's always nice to have a few healthy principles to live by:

---

1. Eat color often. Antioxidants don't stay in our bodies very long, and we are constantly being barraged by damaging free radicals. It seems that nearly everything causes oxidative stress, from pollution, cigarette smoke, and the sun's rays to innocuous-seeming activities like eating, breathing, and exercising. So it's smart to pack some color into your diet daily, preferably with each meal. I like to think of the antioxidants in colorful fruits and vegetables as my own personal security detail.

2. Don't be monochrome. It's easy to get into a routine and just start eating kale salads every day. Yes, kale's great for you, but it's not going to give you a full complement of nutrients. Mix it up! Just like an all-black wardrobe can be boring, so can an all-green diet.

3. Go beyond your comfort zone. Even if the idea of mustard greens really freaks you out, try them once. If you don't like them, you're out less money than you'd pay for a new lipstick. Seems like a good deal to me!

4. Make a date with your kitchen. It's easy to pick up lots of healthy produce, but then deadlines, fatigue, and hungry kids can get the better of you, and those crispy greens start to wilt along with your motivation to cook them. I find that it's just as important to set aside time to cook as it is to have the ingredients on hand. You might need to cook early in the morning, during naptime, or even late at night—whatever works for you. Use your smart phone to block out some time to cook and set an alarm. Seriously! Most of the recipes in this book are great at room temperature or reheated, so it's fine to make them in advance.

5. Move it. I don't care what you do, but work up a sweat at least three times a week for 30 to 45 minutes (60 is ideal). Zumba, power walking, gardening, swimming, snowshoeing—whatever gets that heart pumping. It all counts! And make sure your kids see you in your sweaty workout gear. Just like it's important to have them see you eat your broccoli, you set the best example for your kids by being active.

WHAT ARE ANTIOXIDANTS?

We hear a lot these days about how antioxidants help fight the damage caused by free radicals, but what the heck does that really mean? Think of your body's cells as the parent who is trying to keep things in order, but is countering constant attacks from free radicals, which we can think of as unruly toddlers who bash into the furniture, scuff the floor, and use markers on the walls. Antioxidants work as Mom's helper, sweeping up the various messes and leaving things as they were. Free radicals are formed when certain cells are damaged by oxidation, or exposure to oxygen. Oxidation causes a loss of an electron, which creates instability in a cell. Antioxidants have the ability to lend an electron to the free radicals, making them stable again and unable to cause damage. Oxidative stress is the cumulative damage done by free radicals when they have not been counteracted by antioxidants.

Eating in Color Kitchen Gear

I live in a relatively small apartment in Brooklyn that doesn't have extensive storage space, so I've whittled down my kitchen gear to the essentials. My recipes aren't very complicated and don't require much in the way of fancy kitchen tools. But you will need the following:

Chef's knife: These knives can tackle everything from carving a roast chicken to slicing through a hard winter squash. Since they're an investment, I recommend going to the store to handle them and find the one that's right for the size of your hand and feels balanced. And please wash your knives by hand! Running them through the dishwasher dulls the blade, and you're more likely to cut yourself with a dull knife.

Paring knife: I like using a paring knife for slicing small fruits and doing other, more detailed work.

Bread knife: The serrated blade on these knives make it much easier and safer to cut through crusty bread and bagels.

Kitchen shears: These are super-handy for mincing herbs without bruising them, cutting up long strands of pasta for little eaters, snipping kitchen twine—I could go on and on. Keep them dedicated for kitchen tasks only. If you start using them for paper and such, they'll become dull.

Microplane grater: This is essential for zesting citrus and grating hard cheeses and chocolate. I have several different sizes, but you can get away with the "classic series" zester/grater that was originally used for woodworking.

Two rimmed baking sheets: You'll need a baking sheet to toast nuts, roast vegetables, and bake pizza. One is fine, but it's better to have a pair.

Silpat mat: These are wonderful for baking cookies or making chocolate bark and are amazingly nonstick. You can always use parchment instead, but a Silpat (or other silicon baking mat) is a nice splurge—and you'll have it for years.

A 12-cup muffin pan: For making muffins, of course, but you'll also need them for my mini frittatas (page 102).

Multiple cutting boards: Yes, they take up space, but I find that if I don't have a cutting board that's ready to go, it can derail my dinner plans. Who wants to clean and dry a board before getting started? I keep two large plastic boards, plus a mini plastic one (excellent if you're just slicing a lime or a few garlic cloves), and a wooden board—which only gets used for bread and nuts because I can't disinfect it in the dishwasher.

A 2-quart (2L) saucepan: I find that a 2-quart (2L) saucepan with a lid can handle most recipes, from grains to sauces. It's also nice to have a 6-quart (6L) saucepan when you're making larger quantities or doubling recipes.

Large sauté pan: There's nothing worse than finding that your shrimp or vegetables won't fit into your pan. Okay, there are worse things, but it's annoying to have to cook things in multiple batches if you don't have to. A 10-inch (25.5cm) pan is great, but a 12-inch (30.5cm) is even better. If you have a huge kitchen and lots of storage, go nuts and get both!

Fine-mesh sieve: You'll need one of these for specific recipes like my Matcha Panna Cotta (page 146), but it's also handy for scooping vegetables out of blanching water, rinsing grains, or transferring pasta to a bowl when you don't want to use a colander.

Two colanders: Since most of my recipes call for multiple fruits or vegetables, it's nice to have a couple of colanders on hand. Several companies now make the collapsible kind, so they're easier to store.

Eating in Color Ingredients— A Cheat Sheet

A cook is only as good as the ingredients she has on hand, so make it easy on yourself by staying stocked up on items that help meals come together quickly and add a boost of flavor without much fuss. Here's my go-to list:

Agave nectar: This natural sweetener is made from the blue agave plant. It comes in both light and dark (or amber) varieties, which simply refers to the color of the nectar. Since it has a syruplike consistency, I like using it to sweeten drinks, smoothies, and vinaigrettes. It's also wonderful in marinades and pickling liquid. The texture is similar to honey, but the flavor is more subtle. I love honey, too, but I think agave is more neutral. Since agave is sweeter than sugar, you can use less of it to sweeten things up.

Berries: I go for fresh in the spring and summer and mostly frozen in the fall and winter. I buy organic whenever possible. Berries are a delicious snack, of course, but I also throw the fresh ones into salads for a bit of sparkle. And frozen berries are perfect for smoothies or my Triple Berry Sauce (page 153).

Canned fish, such as tuna or smoked trout (good-quality stuff): These are a no-brainer way to turn a salad or pasta into a main dish.

Chicken sausage: There are so many great companies now making really flavorful and healthy sausages. I keep a few packages on hand for weeknight dinners and throw them into pasta dishes and quiche. If I notice that the sausages are getting dangerously close to their sell-by dates, I just throw them in the freezer.

Chocolate (semisweet), chips, chunks, or bars: When the urge to bake strikes, I like knowing that I don't have to run to the store. I keep my chocolate supplies in the freezer so my husband doesn't snack on them (sorry, honey!).

Dried fruit: I like to keep an assortment around, including apricots, blueberries, cranberries, mangos, raisins, and plums (prunes). They're a great snack to throw into your purse or diaper bag as you're running out the door and can liven up a salad or a grain dish in an instant.

Extra-virgin olive oil: We use extra-virgin olive oil for nearly all our cooking. (I keep canola oil for baking and for cooking certain things like fish, which I don't want to impart a fruity, olive flavor to.) Extra-virgin olive oil is the first press of the olive to extract the oil, so the antioxidant-rich plant phenols are intact. Regular olive oil has gone through several pressings and has fewer health benefits. Since extra-virgin oil is sensitive to heat and light (and it's expensive), I store ours in a metal decanter. If you don't, make sure to keep it in a cupboard that is not next to the stove. If you buy it in bulk like we do, transfer some to a smaller container for everyday use, and put the rest in a cool, dark place.

Garlic: Nothing adds flavor quite like garlic. An unbroken bulb can last up to eight weeks, but check on it weekly to make sure the cloves are not dried out or sprouting.

Grana Padano: In several recipes I call for Parmesan—an informal and general term to refer to an entire family of hard grating cheeses, the most famous of which is Parmigiano-Reggiano. Grana Padano is a deliciously nutty cheese and is very similar in taste and texture to Parmigiano-Reggiano, but generally a few dollars cheaper per pound. And since we use so much of it on pasta and over vegetables, it's a great substitute.

Greek yogurt: I keep plain fat-free as well as 2% plain Greek yogurt on hand for making dips, smoothies, and baked goods. I'll use fat-free in otherwise rich dishes to help lower the saturated fat. Greek yogurt contains two times the amount of protein as regular yogurt because it's made with more milk.

Lemons and limes: Essential for brightening the flavor and color of dishes, making salad dressing and marinades, and enhancing flavor without salt; we keep several of each in the fridge at all times.

Nuts and seeds: I always have almonds, walnuts, pecans, pistachios, pepitas (pumpkin seeds), pine nuts, flax, hemp, and chia seeds on hand. I like to store them in the freezer so they stay fresh longer.

Pasta: I don't need to tell you that pasta makes a quick meal. But I think what's key is having an assortment on hand, like whole-wheat and regular versions of spaghetti and linguini, and penne or rigatoni, plus fun shapes like orecchiette (little ears), farfalle (bowties), campanelle (bell-shaped), gemelli (twists), and chiocciole (snail shells). Switching up the shapes helps combat the boredom that can set in when you serve pasta often.

Quinoa: I keep other grains on hand, too, but quinoa is my go-to when I don't have much time. Unless you're going with instant rice, you really can't beat a 15-minute cook time.

Sea salt: I use sea salt exclusively at home and in all these recipes, unless I'm pickling vegetables or making a roast, and then I'll use kosher salt. Both of these salts have a larger crystal size than regular table salt, which means you need less of them to achieve the same amount of salty flavor. Sea salt and kosher salt also do not contain the additives used in table salt, which gives them a cleaner flavor.

Seasonal fruits and vegetables: I keep two bowls filled with fruit all year round. In the spring and summer, they're brimming with stone fruit like nectarines, peaches, and plums, and in the winter they're loaded with pears and apples. Bananas are a constant. I find that if the fruit is on display, it's more enticing and we're more likely to eat it. The same goes for vegetables—in the summer it's a lot of summer squash, corn, tomatoes, and eggplant. Fall and winter favorites include various winter squash, sweet potatoes, parsnips, and carrots. I try to go through my produce drawers every few days to make sure nothing is languishing.

Shallots: I love onions, but my eyes are super sensitive, so I use shallots in lots of weeknight dishes. They're smaller and easier to peel, so the chopping gets done before my eyes get too watery. And they're sweeter and milder than most onions, so they're a better choice for kids or date night.

Whole-wheat frozen pie crusts: Yes, they're great for pie, but I really keep them around for making quiche. Just whisk up some eggs, throw in some cheese, and add whatever leftover vegetables and meat you might have on hand. Turn to page 48 for a tasty weeknight idea.

Reds

Since at least as far back as Roman times, the color red has signified power and wealth. Studies show that women are more attracted to men wearing red, and we all know the impact of a good red lipstick. This bold and beautiful family of fruits and vegetables is certainly physically attractive, but it also boasts a wide range of heart-healthy nutrients. Many members of the red family contain high levels of the antioxidant vitamin C, potassium, and fiber. Vitamin C helps fight damage caused by pesky free radicals throughout the body. Potassium is essential for maintaining normal blood pressure and keeps your heart beating regularly. And soluble fiber, found in many red fruits, helps lower "bad" LDL cholesterol.

Simply Red Fruit Salad

SERVES 8

I usually like to combine contrasting colors in my fruit salads, but something interesting happened when I decided to go with just red hues. The salad became more like a watercolor painting, with each color bleeding into the other. And with the little jewel-like arils (pomegranate seeds) on top, this salad is not only sweet, it's good-looking, too. It's the perfect ending to a spring or summer meal.

½ cup (70g) DRIED CHERRIES

1 pound (450g) STRAWBERRIES, hulled and quartered (halved if small)

1 cup (110g) RED GRAPES, halved

2 BLOOD or NAVEL ORANGES, depending on the season

Finely grated zest and juice of ½ LIME

1 tablespoon STRAWBERRY JAM

⅓ cup (50g) POMEGRANATE SEEDS (arils) (from 1 pomegranate; see Note)

1. In a small heatproof bowl, combine the cherries and enough boiling water to cover them. Let sit for 15 minutes; drain and reserve the liquid in a large bowl.

2. Add the strawberries and grapes to the bowl with the cherries.

3. Over a bowl, using a sharp paring knife, remove the skin and white pith from the oranges, collecting any juices in the bowl. Use the knife to slice alongside both membranes of each segment, releasing the citrus segments and letting them fall gently into the bowl. Squeeze any remaining juice from the membranes. Transfer the segments to the bowl with the cherries, strawberries, and grapes; reserve the juice.

4. In a small saucepan, combine the reserved liquid from the cherries, the reserved juice from the oranges, and the lime zest and juice. Add the jam and bring to a boil, whisking vigorously to break up the jam. Boil for 3 minutes, until the sauce has reduced by half. Let cool completely at room temperature (chilling will cause the sauce to solidify).

5. Before serving, drizzle the sauce over the fruit and top with the pomegranate arils.

NOTE: See page 22 for instructions on how to extract pomegranate seeds (arils) from the fruit.

CALORIES 99

FAT 0.29g
sat 0.03g
mono 0.03g
poly 0.1g

PROTEIN 1.3g

CARBOHYDRATES 24g

FIBER 5g

CHOLESTEROL 0mg

IRON 0.5mg

SODIUM 1.2mg

POTASSIUM 143mg

CALCIUM 41mg

Goji–Chocolate Chunk Muffins

MAKES 12 MUFFINS

Goji berries have gotten a lot of hype and attention over the past five years. They are rich in antioxidants and vitamin A, and are touted for their immune-boosting and antiaging properties. They're also incredibly expensive, so if you can't find them, or if you don't want to shell out lots of cash for them, substitute chopped dried cherries.

COOKING SPRAY, for the pan

½ cup (55g) dried GOJI BERRIES

1 cup (125g) WHOLE-WHEAT FLOUR

½ cup (60g) ALL-PURPOSE FLOUR

½ cup (30g) WHEAT or OAT BRAN

2 tablespoons toasted WHEAT GERM

½ teaspoon ground CINNAMON

¾ cup (150g) loosely packed LIGHT BROWN SUGAR

½ cup (74g) SEMISWEET CHOCOLATE CHUNKS

2 large EGGS

1 teaspoon pure VANILLA EXTRACT

¾ cup (180ml) 2% MILK

1. Preheat the oven to 350ºF (177ºC). Spray a 12-cup muffin pan with cooking spray.

2. In a small heatproof bowl, combine the goji berries and enough boiling water to cover them. Let sit for 15 minutes. Drain and set aside.

3. In a large bowl, combine the whole-wheat and all-purpose flours, the wheat bran, wheat germ, cinnamon, brown sugar, and chocolate.

4. In another bowl, whisk together the eggs, vanilla, and milk. Stir in the drained berries. Add the wet mixture to the dry mixture and stir until just combined. Scoop the batter into the prepared pan and bake for 20 minutes, until the tops of muffins are golden and dry to the touch. Let cool in the pan for 15 to 20 minutes. Enjoy!

CALORIES 168

FAT 4g
sat 2g
mono 0.5g
poly 0.3g

PROTEIN 5g

CARBOHYDRATES 30g

FIBER 3g

CHOLESTEROL 36mg

IRON 1mg

SODIUM 40mg

POTASSIUM 89mg

CALCIUM 43mg

Strawberries

RECIPES: **Simply Red Fruit Salad,** page 18 **Triple Berry Sauce,** page 153

The basics: This sweet, juicy berry has grown wild for centuries in North America, South America, and Europe. A member of the rose family, strawberries have been cultivated since the thirteenth century.

Seasonality: Strawberry season is from April through September, and that's when you'll find the sweetest ones, but strawberries can be found year-round.

Good stuff: Packed with vitamin C and just 46 calories per cup (144g), strawberries make a wonderful, healthy treat. All those little seeds you see also contribute to the fiber in the berries—1 cup has 3g. The ruby-colored berries are a significant source of folate, which is important for a healthy pregnancy and plays a role in keeping your heart healthy. Strawberries also contain the important electrolyte potassium, which is essential for muscle contractions and also helps keep your heart healthy.

Pick it: Look for brightly colored berries with that delicious berry scent. Avoid berries that appear soft or have any mold on them. They should also be uniformly red and should not have seedy looking tips. The caps should be green and unwilted.

Store it: Strawberries can be kept in the refrigerator for two to three days. If you purchased the berries in a container, keep them in it until you're ready to use them. If you purchased them loose, place them in a single layer on paper towels in the fridge.

Use it: Berries should be washed just before eating them. Delicious raw as a snack, strawberries make a bright addition to salads (both fruity and green), desserts, smoothies, and, of course, jams and compotes.

Pomegranates

RECIPE: **Simply Red Fruit Salad,** page 18

The basics: A symbol of fertility since biblical times, the pomegranate has significance in many of the world's religions. Thanks to its medicinal uses throughout time, pomegranates are part of the coat of arms of several medical associations. The pomegranate grows throughout Asia, the Mediterranean, Africa, India, and California. Inside the pomegranate's ruby case are hundreds of sweet-tart seeds known as arils.

Seasonality: Pomegranates are in season from September through January.

Good stuff: Preliminary research shows that chemicals in pomegranate juice may slow the progression of atherosclerosis (hardening of the arteries) and might help fight cancer. More research is needed, but it's clear that pomegranates contain a high level of the polyphenol antioxidant ellagitannins.

Pick it: Choose pomegranates that are heavy for their size and have a smooth, unblemished skin. If purchasing just the arils—the jewel-like seeds inside the fruit—look for plump ones with a bright ruby color in the refrigerated section of your grocery store.

Store it: Whole pomegranates can last up to a month at room temperature and up to a few months in the refrigerator. They keep best when individually wrapped in paper and stored in a low-humidity compartment in the refrigerator.

Use it: Pomegranates are a bit tricky to tackle, but if you follow these steps you'll get all the tasty seeds out without staining your clothes, hands, or countertops:

1. Slice the fruit in half and then submerge both halves in a bowl of water.

2. Gently use your fingers to remove the cream-colored membranes, releasing the juicy seeds. The seeds will float and the waxy membrane will sink to the bottom of the bowl.

3. Once you've released all the seeds from the membranes, remove and discard the large pieces of the membrane and pour the contents of the bowl into a colander. Using a slotted spoon, you can then gently transfer the seeds to a clean kitchen towel to dry.

You can use the seeds in salads, atop yogurt, or blended into smoothies. Depending on the freshness of the pomegranate, the seeds will last from a few days to a week in the refrigerator. The seeds can be frozen for several months. To freeze, spread the seeds out on a wax paper–lined baking sheet and freeze for two hours. Then transfer to a zip-top plastic bag or other sealed container and return to the freezer.

Ultimate Breakfast Sandwich

SERVES 1

One morning, while my husband and I took turns yawning and pushing our daughter, Willa, on the swing at the playground, I started fantasizing about making the ultimate breakfast sandwich. I asked Jon what would be on his, and it inevitably included sausage and hot sauce. Tasty, sure, but I wanted a combo that was not only satisfyingly yummy, but wouldn't leave me feeling weighed down with unnecessary grease. Herewith, my own ultimate combination, which packs plenty of protein, fiber, and calcium.

COOKING SPRAY, for the pan

1 large EGG, whisked

Pinch of SALT

Pinch of freshly ground BLACK PEPPER

2 slices WHOLE-GRAIN BREAD

1 slice CHEDDAR CHEESE

¼ ripe AVOCADO, peeled and sliced

2 tablespoons ROASTED GRAPE TOMATOES (page 31)

1. Spray a small sauté pan with cooking spray and heat over medium-high heat. Add the egg and move it around the pan with a spatula until scrambled, about 1 minute. Season with the salt and pepper.

2. While the egg cooks, toast the bread to your desired degree of toastiness.

3. Place the cheese on one slice of toast and the avocado slices on the other. Using a table knife, gently spread the avocado across the surface of the bread. Layer the scrambled egg over the cheese and top with the tomatoes. Place the slice of toast with the avocado over the tomatoes and gently press down. Slice in half and daydream about *your* ultimate egg sandwich.

CALORIES 410

FAT 24.6g
sat 9g
mono 7.7g
poly 2g

PROTEIN 18g

CARBOHYDRATES 34g

FIBER 14g

CHOLESTEROL 216mg

IRON 3mg

SODIUM 450mg

POTASSIUM 378mg

CALCIUM 440mg

Watermelon-Cucumber Cooler (aka Hangover Helper)

SERVES 4

I haven't been on a bender since well before I had kids. But sometimes I'll get "overserved" at an event, or a new cocktail might leave me a bit more bleary-eyed than I'd like. That's when I turn to this refreshing concoction. The melon and cucumber help to hydrate you, while the salt and mint aid in settling your stomach.

2 cups (300g) cubed WATERMELON

½ cup (75g) peeled and sliced CUCUMBER, any variety

2 tablespoons fresh LIME JUICE

¼ teaspoon SALT

6 fresh MINT leaves, plus more for garnish

1 liter SPARKLING WATER, chilled

AGAVE NECTAR (light or dark) (optional)

ICE, for serving

1. Combine the watermelon, cucumber, lime juice, salt, and mint in a blender and blend until smooth.

2. Strain the mixture through a fine-mesh sieve, pressing to release all the liquid.

3. Into a tall glass filled with ice, pour ½ cup (125ml) of the watermelon mixture and top with ½ cup (125ml) or more of the sparkling water. Stir in agave to taste, if using. Sip slowly until you've recovered. Have another glass if you need it. Store any remaining cooler covered in the refrigerator for up to 1 day. Stir well before drinking.

CALORIES 57

FAT 0.14g
sat 0.02g
mono 0.03g
poly 0.04g

PROTEIN 0.6g

CARBOHYDRATES 15g

FIBER 0g

CHOLESTEROL 0mg

IRON 0.3mg

SODIUM 199mg

POTASSIUM 120mg

CALCIUM 21mg

Watermelon

RECIPES: **Watermelon-Cucumber Cooler (aka Hangover Helper),** opposite **Watermelon, Cucumber, and Feta Salad with Thyme,** page 27 **Triple Melon Granita,** page 44

The basics: Thought to be originally from Africa, the watermelon is an American favorite. The flesh of this juicy melon is usually a deep pink, but it can also be yellow or even white. Watermelons range from the size of a cantaloupe to a hefty thirty pounds or more. The melons usually contain black seeds, but seedless varieties (which still have a few edible white seeds) have become very common.

Seasonality: You can find them from May through September, but peak watermelon time is mid June to late August.

Good stuff: Consisting of 92 percent water, this hydrating melon deserves its status as a warm-weather staple. It also has earned its chops in the phytonutrient category, with high levels of lycopene. Lycopene is a type of carotenoid that gives watermelon its color. Several studies have found that people with higher amounts of lycopene in their blood have a lower risk of some types of cancer. The evidence is strongest for cancer of the lung, stomach, and prostate. Lycopene may also help protect against cancer of the cervix, breast, mouth, pancreas, esophagus, colon, and rectum. Lycopene content is highest in fully ripe—and very red-pink—melons.

Pick it: A watermelon should feel heavy for its size and have a symmetrical shape. Avoid melons with soft spots or cracks in the rind. If buying a melon that is already halved or sliced, look for the flesh to have a bright color. The surface should not appear dry or grainy.

Store it: Watermelon is best kept in the refrigerator until used, but if you don't have the space, keep it in a cool spot in your kitchen. Once it has been sliced open, store the remaining watermelon in the refrigerator for up to three days, either wrapped tightly in plastic or stored in an airtight container.

Use it: Watermelon is incredibly refreshing eaten in slices and cubes. You can also juice it, use it in smoothies and drinks, or make frozen desserts out of it. It's a refreshing addition to fruit salads. In Asia, watermelon seeds are eaten plain or roasted and salted. Watermelon rind can be pickled.

Radicchio

RECIPE: **Salad in a Jar,** page 33

The basics: As Italian as its name sounds, radicchio is a variety of red chicory. It has a bitter, earthy flavor that helps balance out the richness of many dishes. Radicchio di Chioggia is the most popular variety of radicchio. The head is about the size of a medium orange, and the leaves are a deep maroon with white ribs. The milder radicchio di Treviso grows in longer heads, like endive (and is often referred to as red endive), but has the same coloring on the leaves.

Seasonality: Radicchio is grown year-round, but the peak growing time is from midwinter to early spring.

Good stuff: As with other lettuces, radicchio is very low in calories—1 cup (40g) contains just 9. But it's loaded with the antioxidants zeaxanthin and lutein. Radicchio also contains fructans, which act as a prebiotic in the digestive system and may help reduce the risk of cancer. Prebiotics provide food for probiotics—good bacteria—to grow. Probiotics help maintain a balanced digestive system, support overall health, and may help prevent and treat vaginal yeast infections as well as eczema in children.

Pick it: Look for radicchio heads that are tightly packed with no signs of shriveling or browning.

Store it: Keep radicchio tightly wrapped in the refrigerator for up to five days.

Use it: Remove the core of the radicchio and rinse and dry the leaves before using. You can chop or shred the leaves and use them in salads, as part of a crudité platter, or even as a pizza topping. You can also quarter the heads and grill, roast, or braise them.

Watermelon, Cucumber, and Feta Salad with Thyme

SERVES 4

There's a reason why watermelon and cucumber are such a classic pairing—they're amazing together. The sweet, juicy melon and the crunchy cuke are in fact part of the same plant family, and both are packed with lots of refreshing H_2O. Oh, and this salad is a cool 83 calories per serving, which makes it even more enticing for summertime.

1 cup (150g) peeled and diced seedless CUCUMBER

3 cups (450g) seeded and cubed WATERMELON

½ cup (75g) cubed FETA CHEESE

1 teaspoon fresh THYME leaves

1 tablespoon aged BALSAMIC VINEGAR

¼ teaspoon SALT

¼ teaspoon freshly ground BLACK PEPPER

Fresh BASIL leaves, for garnish (optional)

In a medium serving bowl, gently toss the cucumber, watermelon, feta, thyme, vinegar, salt, and pepper together. Garnish with basil leaves, if using, and serve.

CALORIES 83

FAT 3.3g
sat 1.8g
mono 0.04g
poly 0.06g

PROTEIN 4g

CARBOHYDRATES 11g

FIBER 1g

CHOLESTEROL 10mg

IRON 0.5mg

SODIUM 315mg

POTASSIUM 177mg

CALCIUM 56mg

Hibiscus-Tangelo Iced Tea

SERVES 8

The incredible ruby hue and deliciously tart flavor of this tea are reasons alone to make up a pitcher. But hibiscus is also rich in vitamin C and has been found to help lower blood pressure. Whatever your reason for having a glass, it's a wonderful way to refresh on a warm day.

8 HIBISCUS TEA BAGS

2 TANGELOS

Juice of 1 LIME

AGAVE NECTAR (light or dark) (optional)

ICE, for serving

1. In a saucepan, bring 4 cups (1L) of water to a boil. Add the tea bags and remove the pan from the heat. Let steep until the water becomes a deep ruby color, 10 to 15 minutes. Remove and discard the tea bags.

2. Cut 1 tangelo in half and squeeze the juice from the halves into a small bowl.

3. Pour the tea into a large pitcher and add 4 cups (1L) of cold water, plus the tangelo and lime juices. Add agave nectar to taste, if using. Refrigerate until cold.

4. Cut the remaining tangelo crosswise into 8 wheels. Serve the tea over ice in tall glasses with a slice of tangelo for garnish.

CALORIES 43

FAT 0.1g
sat 0.01g
mono 0.01g
poly 0.02g

PROTEIN 0g

CARBOHYDRATES 11g

FIBER 0g

CHOLESTEROL 0mg

IRON 0mg

SODIUM 0.5mg

POTASSIUM 41mg

CALCIUM 9mg

Beets

RECIPES: **Grilled Shrimp Tacos,** page 38 **Golden Beets with Parsley Pesto and Fregola,** page 91

The basics: The beets we use in salads and other recipes are referred to as the garden beet. There are also sugar beets, which are used to make sugar or are fermented to produce alcohol, and fodder beets, which are used for animal feed. Garden beets come in red, golden, white, and red-and-white-striped ("Chioggia") variations.

Seasonality: Beets are grown year-round.

Good stuff: Beyond their incredible, earthy flavor, beets are also a nutritional powerhouse. Rich in iron, fiber, folic acid (important for a healthy pregnancy and a healthy heart), and potassium, they're an excellent way to boost the nutrition in a salad or pasta dish. And with just 75 calories a cup (150g), they're especially nice when you're keeping an eye on calories.

Pick it: Choose firm beets with smooth skins. If the beet greens are still attached, they should be crisp and bright green.

Store it: Beet greens should be removed from the bulb as soon as you get them home because the greens pull out moisture from the bulb. Trim the beet stem with a knife or kitchen shears to about 1 inch (2.5cm) from the top of the beet—any more and you'll lose nutrients when you cook them. Store the greens separately from the bulb. Beets will keep in a plastic bag in the refrigerator for up to three weeks.

Use it: You can use the beet greens as well as the bulb, but the greens should be cooked within a day of purchasing them. Beets can be boiled, but it's the least flavorful way to cook them. They can be eaten raw if grated, and used in salads or as a garnish. My favorite method of cooking beets is to roast them. Here's how I do it:

1. Preheat the oven to 450°F (232°C).

2. Place trimmed beets in a colander and rinse them really well under running water, using your hands to rub off any soil.

3. Dry gently with paper towels. Do not peel.

4. Wrap the beets tightly in foil and place them in a pie dish or on a rimmed baking sheet. Roast for 1 hour, until the beets are tender and can be pierced easily with a knife. Let cool completely.

5. Once the beets are cool, use a paper towel to rub the skins until they slide off. (You can use your hands, but they will turn pink.)

Roasted beets will keep in the refrigerator for three days. Once you've cooked them, you can do anything you want! Slice them thinly and give them a drizzle of good olive oil, plus a sprinkle of salt and pepper. Or dice them and toss with pasta and ricotta salata. Or cut them into wedges and serve over seasoned grains.

Tomatoes

The basics: A member of the nightshade family, the tomato is the fruit of a vine native to South America. There are dozens of varieties, ranging from the petite grape and cherry tomatoes to the hefty Mortgage Lifters. In addition to commercially grown tomatoes, there are also hundreds of heirloom varieties, which range in shape and color, including green, yellow, and purple. Not everyone agrees on what "heirloom" means, but in general it refers to a plant variety that is at least fifty years old and has not been genetically modified. When they're available, I prefer buying heirloom tomatoes from our local farmer's market over conventional types. The flavor of heirlooms is generally more pronounced, and the shapes and colors are fun. Beyond that, I like supporting the continued farming of these older varieties because they help to ensure genetic diversity. That's important because plants that lack diversity are more susceptible to pathogens and environmental stresses, which can wipe out an entire crop.

Seasonality: Peak tomato season is June through October, depending on region.

Good stuff: One cup (149g) of cherry tomatoes has a mere 27 calories and a substantial amount of beta-carotene. Fresh tomatoes are a good source of the antioxidant lycopene, but our bodies are better able to absorb the lycopene in cooked tomatoes. Lycopene is a type of carotenoid that gives tomatoes their color.

Several studies have found that people with higher amounts of lycopene in their blood have a lower risk of some types of cancer. The evidence is strongest for cancer of the lung, stomach, and prostate. Lycopene may also help protect against cancer of the cervix, breast, mouth, pancreas, esophagus, colon, and rectum.

Pick it: Regardless of color, tomatoes should have a smooth skin without cracks or wrinkles. They should have a fresh, pleasant scent.

Store it: Tomatoes should be kept at room temperature. Cold temperatures damage the fruit and can make it mealy and flavorless. Unripe tomatoes can be ripened at room temperature in a paper bag with an apple. The apple releases ethylene, which helps speed the ripening process. Ripe tomatoes should be used within a few days.

Use it: There is hardly a flavor quite so evocative of summer as a ripe tomato, possibly sprinkled with a few flakes of sea salt. Tomatoes can be used in everything from appetizers and salads to soups, sauces, and main courses. They can be stuffed, grilled, blended, roasted, or fried. Tomatoes can also be dried and stored in olive oil. Studies have found that eating lycopene-rich fruits and vegetables in conjunction with a small amount of oil or fat increases the amount of the nutrient that is absorbed. So slice up a tomato, give it a drizzle of extra-virgin olive oil, and enjoy!

Roasted Grape Tomatoes

SERVES 6

The sweetness of grape tomatoes becomes even more concentrated when you roast them. This go-to side is excellent with chicken, salmon, and juicy grilled steaks. The tomatoes are also a welcome addition to pasta, grain-based salads, and breakfast sandwiches, like the one on page 23.

1 pint (300g) GRAPE or CHERRY TOMATOES, halved

1 large clove GARLIC, sliced thinly

1 tablespoon extra-virgin OLIVE OIL

⅛ teaspoon SALT

⅛ teaspoon freshly ground BLACK PEPPER

1. Preheat the oven to 400ºF (205ºC).

2. Place the tomatoes and garlic in a medium-size glass baking dish, such as a pie plate; toss. Drizzle with the oil and sprinkle with the salt and pepper. Roast for 20 to 23 minutes, until the tomatoes are wrinkled and slightly collapsed. Serve warm or at room temperature. The tomatoes will keep for up to 3 days in an airtight container in the refrigerator.

CALORIES 31

FAT 2.4g
sat 0.3g
mono 1.8g
poly 0.25g

PROTEIN 0.5g

CARBOHYDRATES 2g

FIBER 1g

CHOLESTEROL 0mg

IRON 0.2mg

SODIUM 61mg

POTASSIUM 120mg

CALCIUM 6mg

Salad in a Jar

SERVES 4

I found inspiration for this salad while browsing Pinterest. Not only is it gorgeous, it's the perfect bring-along to work. The genius is in the order that you arrange the ingredients in the jar—make sure the heavy and wet ingredients go on the bottom, and the delicate greens go on top. You can do the same thing with all your favorite salads!

¼ cup (60ml) WALNUT OIL

¼ cup (60ml) CRANBERRY JUICE

1 tablespoon DIJON MUSTARD

1 teaspoon AGAVE NECTAR
(light or dark)

2 teaspoons RED WINE VINEGAR

⅛ teaspoon SALT

⅛ teaspoon freshly ground BLACK PEPPER

1 teaspoon chopped fresh TARRAGON leaves (optional)

1 (15-ounce/420g) can GARBANZO BEANS, rinsed and drained

½ cup (3 ounces/85g) crumbled French FETA CHEESE

¼ cup (50g) dried CRANBERRIES

1 head RADICCHIO, sliced crosswise into ribbons

½ head RED LEAF LETTUCE, chopped

1. In a medium bowl, whisk together the oil, cranberry juice, mustard, agave nectar, vinegar, salt, and pepper. Stir in the tarragon, if using. Place the beans in the bowl with the dressing, stir to coat, and set aside.

2. If creating jar salads, assemble the salad as follows:

• Place ¼ cup (60g) of the bean mixture in the bottom of a tall mason jar. Follow with 2 tablespoons feta, 1 tablespoon cranberries, one-quarter of the radicchio, and one-quarter of the red leaf lettuce. Repeat with the remaining jars.

If making one large tossed salad, arrange as follows:
• Place the radicchio and red leaf lettuce in a large bowl. Top with the feta, cranberries, and bean mixture. Toss gently to combine.

CALORIES 331

FAT 18.6g
sat 4g
mono 4g
poly 8.8g

PROTEIN 9g

CARBOHYDRATES 32g

FIBER 5g

CHOLESTEROL 17mg

IRON 1.8mg

SODIUM 428mg

POTASSIUM 412mg

CALCIUM 155mg

Classic Marinara
with Zucchini

SERVES 6

Even though we eat an enormous amount of pasta with red sauce in our house, I hadn't made homemade marinara until a few years ago. My German mother never made it, and I guess I thought it was something that was just too much trouble to make from scratch. But while testing a recipe for a magazine I worked for at the time, I realized that homemade sauce is really quite simple. The most time-consuming step is blanching and peeling the tomatoes. If you're really against that, you can always use a 28-ounce (794g) can of whole, peeled tomatoes in their juices, but give the fresh ones a try. I guarantee you'll think it's worth it.

3 pounds (1.3kg) TOMATOES, scored with an X on the bottom

2 tablespoons extra-virgin OLIVE OIL

2 cloves GARLIC, smashed and peeled

1 small ONION, diced

1 medium ZUCCHINI (about 10 ounces/280g), diced

¼ teaspoon SALT

1 teaspoon loosely packed DARK BROWN SUGAR

1. Bring a large pot of water to a boil. Add the tomatoes to the water and boil for 1 minute. Using a slotted spoon, transfer the tomatoes to a plate and let cool. When cool enough to handle, remove their skins and core them. Place the tomatoes in a large bowl and purée them using an immersion blender, or transfer them to a blender and blend until smooth.

2. Heat the olive oil in a large saucepan over medium-high heat. Add the garlic and onion and cook for 4 minutes, until translucent. Reduce the heat to medium. Add the zucchini and salt and cook for 3 minutes more. Add the tomato purée to the pan and simmer until thickened, for 40 minutes. Use immediately or let cool and refrigerate in an airtight container for up to 5 days.

CALORIES 101

FAT 5.3g
sat 0.8g
mono 3.7g
poly 0.7g

PROTEIN 4g

CARBOHYDRATES 12g

FIBER 3.5g

CHOLESTEROL 0mg

IRON 1mg

SODIUM 110mg

POTASSIUM 776mg

CALCIUM 38mg

Radishes

RECIPES: **Grilled Shrimp Tacos,** page 38 **Kale Salad with Watermelon Radishes,** page 111 **Spicy Brown Rice Bowl with Chard,** page 134

The basics: The root of a plant in the mustard family, the radish is a part of the cruciferous family of vegetables. There are several radish varieties, including the gorgeous watermelon radish and the large white daikon radish. The size of radishes can range from as small as a cherry to as large or larger than a carrot, and they can be globe-shaped or elongated. Their color can be white, red, pink, purple, or even black. Watermelon radishes, as the name implies, are green on the outside and bright fuchsia on the inside. Bordeaux radishes are purple and white. Radishes may be mildly peppery to intensely strong depending on the variety and how fresh the radish is. The peppery heat is produced by an enzyme in the radish's skin.

Seasonality: Typical red-skinned globe radishes are grown year-round. The other varieties vary.

Good stuff: A true calorie bargain at just 19 per cup (120g) of sliced radishes, the radish is also packed with phytonutrients, as are its cousins in the cruciferous family, broccoli and cabbage.

Pick it: Look for firm radishes with smooth, unblemished skin and firm roots.

Store it: Refrigerate whole radishes in a plastic bag for up to one month.

Use it: If very fresh and still bright green, radish leaves can be washed well and used as you would spinach. If not using the leaves, remove and discard them, trim the root ends of the radishes, and wash them under running water. To make them extra crunchy, place whole radishes in an ice bath for an hour or more before serving. Radishes are delicious whole, or served like the French do, with good unsalted butter, a sprinkle of salt, and perhaps a baguette. Radishes are lovely in salads, sliced on sandwiches, or grated to add flavor to various dishes. You can even cook radishes and add them to pasta dishes, soups, and stir-fries.

What Are Phytonutrients?

Phytonutrients (also referred to as phytochemicals) are plant compounds that provide a health benefit. Fruits, vegetables, whole grains, legumes, nuts, and seeds are all sources of phytonutrients. Classes of phytonutrients include terpenes, phytosterols, carotenoids, and limonoids.

Rhubarb

RECIPES: **Rhubarb-Plum Syrup,** opposite **Ruby Sparkler,** page 51

The basics: Though it's usually eaten as a fruit, rhubarb is actually a vegetable that belongs to the same family as sorrel and buckwheat. Only the stalks of the plant are edible; the leaves contain oxalic acid and are toxic. There are both hothouse and field varieties. The former has pink stalks while the latter has bright red stalks.

Seasonality: Hothouse rhubarb is grown from December to March. The field variety grows from March to October.

Good stuff: One cup (122g) of the raw tart stuff has 26 calories, 2g of fiber, and offers as much potassium as a cup of milk.

Pick it: Look for rhubarb stalks that are firm and have either a nice pink or red color. If the leaves are still attached, they should be crisp and green.

Store it: Store rhubarb tightly wrapped in a plastic bag in the refrigerator for three to five days.

Use it: If you've ever bitten into a stalk, you know it's incredibly tart. But it has a wonderful texture and pairs well with dried fruit and sweet, fresh fruits like strawberries and apples. In England rhubarb is often paired with ginger. Once you've removed and discarded the leaves, wash the stalks and cut them into 1-inch (2.5cm) pieces. You can then cook it with other ingredients. Rhubarb can also be used in savory dishes.

Rhubarb-Plum Syrup

MAKES 2 CUPS (500ML) SYRUP

Rhubarb grew wild in my mother's garden. Growing up, I remember plucking gigantic stalks and munching them right out of the ground while my mom laughed. Rightly so—I'm sure my face was twisted into a pucker from the vegetable's significant tang. These days I prefer my rhubarb mixed with some sweetness. This pretty syrup makes a lovely spring spritzer with sparkling water or an elegant cocktail, like the Ruby Sparkler on page 51.

1 cup (122g) diced RHUBARB (from about 2 stalks)

1 ripe PLUM, pitted and sliced into wedges

1 cup (250ml) light AGAVE NECTAR

1. In a medium saucepan, combine all of the ingredients. Add 1¼ cups (300ml) of water and bring to a boil over high heat, stirring occasionally. Reduce to a simmer and cook until the syrup is bright red and the fruit has fallen apart, about 5 minutes.

2. Pour the syrup through a fine-mesh sieve, catching the strained syrup in a bowl below. (The fruit can be discarded or eaten—I hate to waste!) Allow the syrup to cool and then transfer it to a clean glass jar with a tightly fitting lid. Refrigerate for up to 2 weeks.

(per 2 ounces)

CALORIES 64

FAT 0g
sat 0g
mono 0g
poly 0g

PROTEIN 0g

CARBOHYDRATES 17g

FIBER 0g

CHOLESTEROL 0mg

IRON 0mg

SODIUM 1mg

POTASSIUM 28mg

CALCIUM 8mg

Grilled Shrimp Tacos

MAKES 8 TACOS; SERVES 4

I first discovered seafood tacos on a trip to San Diego. I was amazed that you could get fish tacos at a fast food restaurant chain called Rubio's and that you could enjoy them on the beach, just steps away. Part of the West Coast approach to cuisine is a casual entertaining style, and these shrimp tacos are ideal for feeding a crowd. Simply set out the prepped ingredients in small bowls and let your family and friends build their own colorful plates.

⅓ cup (50g) peeled and grated fresh BEET (from 1 medium beet)

1 tablespoon SHERRY VINEGAR

1 AVOCADO, pitted, peeled, and cubed

½ cup (80g) diced RED BELL PEPPER

½ cup (60g) thinly sliced RADISH (from 4 radishes)

½ cup (55g) crumbled QUESO FRESCO

½ cup (20g) fresh CILANTRO leaves

2 LIMES, cut into 8 wedges each, for serving

1 pound (450g) medium SHRIMP, peeled and deveined

⅛ teaspoon SALT

⅛ teaspoon freshly ground BLACK PEPPER

¼ teaspoon ground CUMIN

¼ teaspoon CHILI POWDER

1 tablespoon OLIVE OIL, plus more for the pan

8 (6-inch/15cm) CORN TORTILLAS (see Note)

1. In a small bowl, combine the grated beet with the vinegar. Stir to evenly coat the beet with the vinegar.

2. Arrange the beet, avocado, bell pepper, radish, cheese, cilantro, and lime wedges in small individual bowls.

3. In a medium bowl, combine the shrimp with the salt, pepper, cumin, chili powder, and oil. Toss the shrimp in the seasoning to evenly coat.

4. Heat a grill pan over high heat. When it's hot, oil the pan. Add the shrimp and raise the heat to medium-high. Cook the shrimp for 2 to 3 minutes on each side, until opaque. Transfer them to a serving bowl.

5. While the shrimp are cooking, heat the tortillas individually in a dry pan for 30 to 60 seconds each, or in a stack in the oven at 200°F (93°C) until they are warmed through, about 15 minutes. Stack the warmed tortillas and wrap them in a clean kitchen towel; serve in a basket.

6. Grab a plate and build your tacos!

NOTE: I like to use La Tortilla Factory Artisan Tortillas because they are fairly easy to find and their texture is more like homemade tortillas than most store-bought varieties.

CALORIES 405

FAT 17g
sat 3.3g
mono 4.5g
poly 1.5g

PROTEIN 23g

CARBOHYDRATES 42g

FIBER 8g

CHOLESTEROL 153mg

IRON 1mg

SODIUM 853mg

POTASSIUM 580mg

CALCIUM 175mg

Spiced and Spiked Cranberry Cider

SERVES 6

Despite all the wonderful flavors and scents of fall, I've never been a big fan of the season. I think it has always signaled an end of fun for me, and of course it means shorter days and added layers of clothes. But one thing I've always loved about fall is apple cider. As long as I have a steaming mug of it (preferably spiked!), I can brave those chilly autumn nights with a smile. This cider can also be made without the rum, and kids love it as a treat.

4 cups (1L) APPLE CIDER

2 cups (500ml) sweetened CRANBERRY JUICE blend (100 percent juice)

2 CINNAMON STICKS

1 ORANGE, sliced crosswise into wheels

6 ounces (180ml) RUM

1. In a medium saucepan, combine the cider, cranberry juice, cinnamon sticks, and orange wheels. Bring to a boil, then reduce the heat to medium-low and simmer for 20 minutes.

2. Strain the mixture (careful, it's hot!) through a fine-mesh sieve to remove the solids. Add 1 ounce (30ml) of rum per 1 cup (250ml) serving. Curl up in front of the fire and enjoy.

CALORIES 191

FAT 0.04g
sat 0g
mono 0.01g
poly 0.01g

PROTEIN 0.5g

CARBOHYDRATES 32g

FIBER 1g

CHOLESTEROL 0mg

IRON 0.4mg

SODIUM 19mg

POTASSIUM 134mg

CALCIUM 19mg

Cranberries

RECIPES: **Salad in a Jar,** page 33 **Spiced and Spiked Cranberry Cider,** opposite **Cran-Apple Tart Tatin,** page 43

The basics: Used by Native Americans for fabric dye, food, and medicine, the cranberry is one of just three fruits that originated in the United States. German and Dutch settlers noticed that the flower of the cranberry looked like the head and bill of a crane, and thus called the fruit a "crane berry." The berries are grown on shrubs in bogs in Massachusetts, Oregon, Washington, and Wisconsin. The bogs are flooded to harvest the berries, which float.

Seasonality: Cranberries are harvested in the fall and are available fresh through December.

Good stuff: Pleasantly tart and a good source of vitamin C, cranberries are beneficial as a year-round immune booster. In particular, they have the unique ability to prevent certain bacteria from sticking to the lining of the urinary tract, which helps prevent urinary tract infections. This antimicrobial effect is also why cranberries show promise in helping prevent cavities and periodontal disease.

Pick it: Fresh cranberries should be shiny and red. If you find any that look deflated or are discolored or shriveled, discard them.

Store it: Fresh berries can last in the refrigerator in an unopened package for up to two weeks. You can freeze berries in their original plastic bag or in a zip-top plastic bag for up to a year.

Use it: Rinse fresh berries before using them. If you're using frozen cranberries, do not thaw them. Simply add them to the recipe as directed. Because they are so tart, cranberries are usually combined with sweeter fruits in desserts, sauces, and chutneys. They play well with citrus, apples, and pears. Fresh berries are also great in baked goods like muffins and quick breads, which have enough sweetness to balance the berries' pucker. Dried cranberries can also be used in many recipes, and the juice works well in salad dressings, drinks, and sauces.

Apples

The basics: This iconic fruit is a symbol of health and is likely originally from southwestern Asia. There are hundreds of apple varieties ranging in color from red to pink to yellow to green, and ranging in flavor from sweet to tart and everywhere in between.

Seasonality: While you can buy apples year-round, they are most delicious in the fall when they're just harvested.

Good stuff: Crunchy and convenient, apples are a go-to healthy snack. They're low in calories (a medium one has 95) and high in fiber (over 4g), and are associated with a laundry list of health benefits. They contain the flavonoid quercetin, which shows promise for its ability to protect brain neurons from oxidative damage, a known cause of Alzheimer's and Parkinson's diseases. Quercetin also appears to play a role in preventing cancer of the pancreas and prostate. Pectin, a soluble fiber in apple peel, may help boost immunity and improve gut health. Apples help you feel full, which means you'll eat fewer calories if you snack on them about 15 minutes before a meal.

Pick it: Look for apples with smooth skin that's free of bruises and nicks. Depending on whether you're using the apples for cooking or snacking, you'll want to choose the appropriate variety. Apple varieties that are great for both snacking and cooking include Braeburn, Cortland, Fuji, Granny Smith, Jonagold, Lady Apples, McIntosh, and Winesap.

Store it: Keep apples in a cool, dark place. They can sit at room temperature for a few days, but they're best kept in a plastic bag in the refrigerator for a few weeks.

Use it: Rinse apples well just before eating. Most apples are wonderful as a snack, and their culinary uses are numerous. They can add sweetness to salads and to cooked vegetable dishes and purees. Apples also make delicious pies, tarts, and muffins, and can be cooked down into applesauce and apple butter.

Cran-Apple Tart Tatin

SERVES 8

This upside–down tart makes an impressive finish to any fall meal. Just don't leave the leftovers on the table. My dog, Millie, managed to snag and devour at least one-quarter of my tart. While there are special (and expensive) pans made specifically for making tart tatin, you can use any shallow, ovenproof pan.

1 sheet frozen PUFF PASTRY, defrosted

1 teaspoon plus 1 tablespoon UNSALTED BUTTER

½ cup (100g) packed DARK BROWN SUGAR

1½ cups (150g) fresh or frozen CRANBERRIES

2 pounds (900g) GALA or FUJI APPLES (about 4 apples), peeled, cored, and sliced thinly

1 teaspoon ground CINNAMON

1. Preheat the oven to 400ºF (205ºC). Place the puff pastry on a piece of waxed paper, and roll it out into a 10- or 12-inch (25.5 or 30.5cm) circle (depending on the size of your pan); chill in the fridge until ready to use.

2. Place a 10- or 12-inch (25.5 or 30.5cm) cast-iron or other ovenproof pan on the stovetop. Coat the bottom and sides of the pan with 1 teaspoon of the butter. Add the brown sugar in an even layer and top with the cranberries. Add the apple slices in concentric circles, starting with the outside edge of the pan. Make 2 layers of apples (you may have about ¼ of an apple left over), sprinkling the cinnamon on the apples in between the layers.

3. Turn the heat to medium-high and cook for 15 minutes. The cranberries will release their juices. Transfer the pan to the oven and cook 15 minutes more. Remove from the oven, dot with the remaining 1 tablespoon butter, and place the puff pastry over the apples. Remember—your pan is very hot!

4. Return the pan to the oven and bake for 30 minutes more, until the pastry is golden. Let cool for 15 to 20 minutes. Loosen the edges of the tart slightly with a spatula. Place a large plate or platter facedown over the tart and invert the pan onto the plate. Transfer any cranberries left in the pan to the top of the tart. Slice into 8 wedges and serve. It's excellent with vanilla ice cream, of course!

CALORIES 213

FAT 7.2g
sat 3.8g
mono 1.4g
poly 0.3g

PROTEIN 1g

CARBOHYDRATES 40g

FIBER 6g

CHOLESTEROL 14mg

IRON 0.6mg

SODIUM 36mg

POTASSIUM 200mg

CALCIUM 25mg

Triple Melon Granita

SERVES 6

A bit of effort goes into making granita, but on a sweltering summer day, you'll find the reward is well worth the wait.

4 cups (600g) seeded and cubed WATERMELON

1 cup (160g) cubed ORANGE-FLESHED MELON, such as Sugar Kiss or cantaloupe

2 cups (330g) cubed WHITE- or GREEN-FLESHED MELON, such as Galia or honeydew

1 teaspoon finely grated LIME ZEST

5 tablespoons fresh LIME JUICE

2 tablespoons AGAVE NECTAR (light or dark), or more as needed

1. Place a 9-by-13-inch (23 by 33cm) baking dish in the freezer.

2. In a food processor or blender, blend the melons with the lime zest and juice until smooth. Add the agave nectar and blend to combine. Taste and add more agave nectar as needed to suit your preference. Remove the pan from the freezer, pour the melon mixture into it, and return the pan to the freezer.

3. After 1½ hours, remove the pan from the freezer and scrape the granita with a large fork. The mixture will be very slushy at this point; return it to the freezer. Scrape the mixture every 30 minutes, for about 2½ to 3 hours total; it will have a fluffy, flaky texture.

4. Serve the granita in small cups or dessert bowls. Once frozen, granita can be transferred to an airtight container and kept in the freezer for about 1 week.

CALORIES 83

FAT 0.29g
sat 0.05g
mono 0.04g
poly 0.11g

PROTEIN 1.2g

CARBOHYDRATES 21g

FIBER 1g

CHOLESTEROL 0mg

IRON 0.4mg

SODIUM 16mg

POTASSIUM 329mg

CALCIUM 15mg

Cherries

The basics: Like apricots and plums, cherries are part of the stone fruit family. There are about 1,000 cherry varieties, which can be divided into two main groups—sweet and tart cherries. Sweet cherry varieties include Bing, Rainier, Lambert, and Royal Ann. Tart cherries are generally smaller and include Montmorency, Balaton, Richmond, and English Morello. Tart cherries are generally found dried, frozen, or as juice, instead of as fresh fruit. Cherries range in color from the light yellow and pink blushed Rainier to the deeply red Bing. In the United States cherries are grown in California, Michigan, New York, Oregon, Utah, and Washington. They are also imported from Chile.

Seasonality: The short fresh cherry season lasts from May through August. Dried and frozen cherries can be found year-round.

Good stuff: A sweet summer favorite, cherries are a healthy treat on their own. One cup (155g) of pitted cherries has 127 calories, 3g fiber, and 342mg of potassium—about as much as a small banana. Sweet cherries also contain quercetin, hydroxycinnamic acid, and anthocyanins, a type of phytonutrient that gives cherries their deep red color and has anti-inflammatory benefits.

Together, these plant compounds have been shown to reduce oxidative stress and may therefore reduce the risk of Alzheimer's disease. Tart cherries have fewer calories due to their lower sugar content, and studies show they are also rich in anthocyanins. Tart cherries have been shown to help reduce pain from arthritis and post-exercise soreness and are a source of melatonin, a hormone that helps promote healthy sleep patterns.

Pick it: Look for plump, glossy, firm cherries. Avoid cherries that are wrinkled, soft, or are leaking juice.

Store it: Cherries should be refrigerated in a plastic bag until ready to eat. Rinse them just before serving. Cherries will last about three days in the refrigerator; fruit with stems attached will last longer.

Use it: I love a late afternoon bowl of fresh cherries enjoyed just as is. But they're also wonderful in fruit salads, cocktails, ice cream, and baked desserts like clafoutis, pies, cakes, and jam. A natural in sweet recipes, cherries also lend a nice counterpoint in green salads and dishes made with pork, duck, and other poultry. Dried cherries are delicious in cookies, muffins, biscotti, and trail mix.

Raspberries

RECIPES: **Berry-Nectarine Trifle,** page 52 **Matcha Panna Cotta,** page 146 **Triple Berry Sauce,** page 153 **Three-Berry Oat Bars,** page 155

The basics: Raspberries grow on a bramble bush that may originate from southeast Asia. Red raspberries are most popular, but you can also find golden and black varieties. The berries are made of several connecting drupelets surrounding a hollow core. The berries have tiny hairs on them called "styles," which are part of the plant's natural defense mechanism.

Seasonality: The peak season for raspberries is May through September.

Good stuff: Sweet, slightly tart, and intensely flavorful, raspberries are a summer delight. A 1-cup (123g) serving has 64 calories and is packed with 8g of fiber. Raspberries are a good source of vitamin C and folate.

Pick it: Raspberries should be plump, glossy, and free of mold and bruises. The berries should not have the hulls attached. An attached hull indicates that the berry was picked too soon.

Store it: Raspberries are extremely fragile. Keep the berries in their original container and refrigerate them as soon as possible. They will last for one to two days in the fridge.

Use it: Rinse the berries gently just before using them. Raspberries make a delightful snack and are wonderful in all types of desserts and drinks. For making a berry sauce, I find that frozen raspberries are just as tasty and a lot more economical. Raspberries and blackberries can also be enjoyed lightly smashed with some sugar or agave nectar and served with a dollop of crème fraîche or vanilla ice cream.

White Summer Fruit Sangria

SERVES 10

I've always found sangria to be a bit too boozy. I think it's because in addition to the wine, it's usually made with brandy or cognac, plus added sugar. This version is light (only 85 calories!) and refreshing and just perfect for a warm evening out on the terrace.

2 WHITE PEACHES, pitted and sliced into wedges

1 LEMON, sliced crosswise into wheels

1 cup (110g) GREEN GRAPES, halved

1 cup (140g) CHERRIES, pitted

1 bottle dry WHITE WINE, such as Pinot Blanc

3 sprigs fresh MINT

ICE, for serving

1 liter plain SPARKLING WATER

1. Place the fruit into a large (at least 7-cup/1.75L capacity) pitcher and pour the wine over the top. Add the mint and refrigerate for at least 3 hours.

2. To serve, fill large glasses with ice. Pour 5 ounces (148ml) of the sangria into each glass, then top each drink with 2 to 3 ounces (59 to 89ml) of the sparkling water.

CALORIES 85

FAT 0.13g
sat 0.02g
mono 0.02g
poly 0.04g

PROTEIN 0.5g

CARBOHYDRATES 8g

FIBER 0.8g

CHOLESTEROL 0mg

IRON 0.2mg

SODIUM 0.5mg

POTASSIUM 100mg

CALCIUM 6mg

Cherry Tomato, Sausage, and Quinoa Tart

SERVES 6

Every time I make quinoa, I always seem to have a lot left over. It's lovely as a breakfast cereal or in muffins, but I also find that it adds substance to eggy dishes like this tart. This recipe is an easy way to introduce this grain to the quinoa novice. The quinoa actually sinks to the bottom of the crust and you hardly know it's there. And this is a great dish for vegetarians—just skip the sausage.

1 tablespoon grated PARMESAN

1 (9-inch/23cm) frozen whole-wheat PIE SHELL

5 large eggs

½ cup (125ml) 2% MILK

¼ teaspoon SALT

¼ teaspoon freshly ground BLACK PEPPER

⅓ cup (31g) grated MANCHEGO

½ cup (70g) cooked QUINOA (see page 202)

1 link SWEET ITALIAN CHICKEN SAUSAGE, quartered and sliced crosswise into ¼-inch (6mm) pieces

1 cup (150g) CHERRY TOMATOES

1. Preheat the oven to 375ºF (190ºC).

2. Sprinkle the Parmesan over the bottom of the pie shell; set aside.

3. In a large bowl, whisk the eggs together. Add the milk, salt, pepper, cheese, and quinoa and whisk again. Stir in the sausage. Pour the egg mixture into the pie shell. Add the cherry tomatoes to the tart, distributing them evenly, and bake for 40 to 45 minutes, until the tart is set and the top is golden. Cut into 6 wedges and serve.

CALORIES 323

FAT 22g
sat 11g
mono 2g
poly 1g

PROTEIN 13g

CARBOHYDRATES 18g

FIBER 3g

CHOLESTEROL 183mg

IRON 1mg

SODIUM 449mg

POTASSIUM 173mg

CALCIUM 70mg

Peppadew Pops

MAKES 40 POPS; SERVES 20

Peppadew peppers are a fairly recent addition to American grocery store shelves. The peppadew is a variety of piquante pepper that grows in South Africa. They come in mild and hot and red and golden varieties (any would be great in this recipe), and their peppy flavor is a tangy combination of sweet and hot.

1 (14-ounce/440g) jar whole sweet PEPPADEW PEPPERS, drained

8 ounces (225g) GOAT CHEESE, herbed or plain, at room temperature

2 tablespoons 2% MILK

1 large hothouse (English) CUCUMBER, cubed

1. Place the peppers on a serving platter or large plate; set aside.

2. In a small bowl, mix the cheese with the milk, and then transfer the mixture to a zip-top bag. Snip off one of the bottom corners of the bag and pipe a little of the cheese into each of the peppers.

3. Skewer one cucumber cube and then one filled pepper, crosswise, onto a 4- to 5-inch (10 to 12.75cm) wooden skewer or toothpick. Repeat with the remaining cucumber cubes and peppers. Open up a bottle of bubbly and have fun!

CALORIES 56

FAT 3.4g
sat 2.4g
mono 0.8g
poly 0.1g

PROTEIN 3g

CARBOHYDRATES 3g

FIBER 0g

CHOLESTEROL 9mg

IRON 0mg

SODIUM 83mg

POTASSIUM 20mg

CALCIUM 36mg

Ruby Sparkler

MAKES 1 (6-OUNCE/180ML) COCKTAIL

While I love cocktails, I'm no mixologist and usually go for simple combinations, preferably with bubbly. And if the drink is gorgeous to look at while you sip, like this one, that's even better.

2 ounces (60ml) RHUBARB-PLUM SYRUP (see page 37)

1 tablespoon ST. GERMAIN LIQUEUR

4 ounces (125ml) chilled PROSECCO or CAVA

Pour the rhubarb syrup into a Champagne flute. Add the St. Germain and slowly pour in the prosecco or cava. Toast to a lovely occasion!

CALORIES 187

FAT 0g
sat 0g
mono 0g
poly 0g

PROTEIN 0.2g

CARBOHYDRATES 14g

FIBER 0g

CHOLESTEROL 0mg

IRON 0.5mg

SODIUM 9mg

POTASSIUM 126mg

CALCIUM 17mg

Berry-Nectarine Trifle

SERVES 12

A trifle is a traditional English dessert made with layers of cake (sometimes doused with booze), jam, custard, fresh fruit, and whipped cream. My version has less sugar and fat, but still provides a wonderful mix of creamy custard, tender cake, and juicy fruit. If you don't have time to make the Meyer Lemon Pound Cake on page 96, you can use a store-bought pound cake.

For the lemon crème:
1 large EGG

½ cup (100g) SUGAR

1 tablespoon plus 2 teaspoons CORNSTARCH

1¼ cups (300ml) 2% MILK

1 teaspoon pure VANILLA EXTRACT

2 tablespoons fresh LEMON JUICE

1 cup (230g) 2% PLAIN GREEK YOGURT

For the assembly:
12 ounces (340g) RASPBERRIES or other berries

2 WHITE NECTARINES, regular nectarines, or peaches, pitted and sliced

¼ cup (50g) SUGAR

1 MEYER LEMON POUND CAKE ends removed, cut into ½-inch (1.25cm) slices

¼ cup (60ml) GRAND MARNIER LIQUEUR (optional)

1. Make the lemon crème: Whisk the egg in a small bowl and set aside. In a small saucepan, combine the sugar and cornstarch and set over medium-high heat. Gradually whisk in the milk, a little at a time. Bring the mixture to a boil and cook for 1 minute. Remove from the heat.

2. Slowly pour half of the hot milk mixture into the bowl with the egg, stirring, to temper the egg. Pour the egg-milk mixture back into the remaining milk in the saucepan; whisk. Reduce the heat to medium and cook for 2 minutes, whisking until thick. Remove from the heat and stir in the vanilla and lemon juice. Transfer to a small bowl and cover the surface directly with plastic wrap. Chill for 45 minutes, then fold in the yogurt.

3. Combine the fruits and sugar in a bowl. Spread ½ cup (125ml) of the crème onto the bottom of a medium glass bowl or trifle dish. Next layer 5 or 6 slices of the cake over the crème. If using the Grand Marnier, drizzle half over the cake. Distribute half of the fruit on top and follow that with another ½ cup (125ml) of the crème. Add another layer of cake (you may have leftover cake), drizzle with the remaining Grand Marnier, and cover with the remaining berries and crème. Cover and refrigerate for 3 hours or until ready to serve.

CALORIES 335

FAT 10.1g
sat 5.8g
mono 2.3g
poly 0.7g

PROTEIN 8g

CARBOHYDRATES 55g

FIBER 3g

CHOLESTEROL 73mg

IRON 0.7mg

SODIUM 182mg

POTASSIUM 240mg

CALCIUM 117mg

Oranges

Including sweet summer gems like apricots and peaches, as well as robust fall favorites like pumpkin and butternut squash, the orange family is as varied as yours probably is. But one thing they all have in common is a very special nutrient, beta-carotene. You'll read more about this sight-saving and immune-boosting antioxidant in the following pages. Who couldn't use a little dose of sunshine in their bowl?

Spice Girl Pumpkin Muffins

MAKES 12 MUFFINS

If you ever need to sell your home, whip up a batch of these muffins before the open house. The scent of all the warm fall spices creates a cozy atmosphere that's worth almost as much as a good home stager. Plus, these muffins are amazingly moist, with absolutely no oil or butter, making them even more magical.

COOKING SPRAY, for the liners

2 ripe BANANAS, mashed

1 cup (225g) canned PUMPKIN PURÉE

2 large EGGS, whisked

⅓ cup (65g) SUGAR

½ cup (125ml) pure MAPLE SYRUP

2 cups (240g) WHITE WHOLE-WHEAT FLOUR (or half all-purpose flour and half whole-wheat flour)

¼ cup (60g) ground FLAXSEED or CHIA SEED

¼ cup (30g) WHEAT GERM

1 teaspoon BAKING POWDER

1 teaspoon BAKING SODA

½ teaspoon SALT

¼ teaspoon ground CARDAMOM

¼ teaspoon ground NUTMEG

¼ teaspoon ground CLOVES

1 teaspoon ground CINNAMON

¾ cup (114g) SEMISWEET CHOCOLATE CHUNKS (optional)

¼ cup (35g) shelled raw PUMPKIN SEEDS

1. Preheat the oven to 375ºF (190ºC). Line a 12-cup muffin pan with liners. Spray the liners with cooking spray.

2. In a large bowl, mix together the bananas, pumpkin, eggs, sugar, and maple syrup.

3. In a medium bowl, mix together the flour, flaxseed, wheat germ, baking powder, baking soda, salt, cardamom, nutmeg, cloves, and cinnamon.

4. Gently stir the wet ingredients into the dry. Do not overmix.

5. Stir in the chocolate chunks, if using (silly not to!).

6. Use a ⅓-cup (80ml) measure to fill the muffin liners (you'll have a bit of batter left over). Sprinkle the pumpkin seeds evenly over muffins.

7. Bake for 20 minutes, until the tops feel dry when touched. Transfer the muffins to a baking rack to cool.

CALORIES 238

FAT 6g
sat 2g
mono 0.8g
poly 1g

PROTEIN 7g

CARBOHYDRATES 42g

FIBER 5g

CHOLESTEROL 31mg

IRON 1.7mg

SODIUM 266mg

POTASSIUM 223mg

CALCIUM 51mg

Coco-Mango Smoothie

SERVES 2

Byron Bay is a beach town south of Brisbane, Australia. I had the good fortune to spend a few days there during a six-month stint in the country in my early twenties. It was the perfect time to hang out with surfers and learn the proper way to cut up a mango: Using your pocket knife (or a sharp paring knife), remove the outer sides or "cheeks" of the mango, cutting fairly close to the seed, but avoiding the fibrous part of the fruit in the center. Use your knife to create a crosshatch pattern in the flesh of the cheeks, and then slice the resulting cubes into your mouth. Well, at least that's what you do when you're at the beach! It doesn't matter if mango juice runs down your chin because the ever-present ocean is there to clean you up in a jiff, mate. Turmeric intensifies the color of the shake and also offers anti-inflammatory benefits, so it's great post workout. To boost the protein in this vegan smoothie, you can add a scoop of protein powder made from plant protein (see Resources, page 214).

1 large ripe MANGO, peeled, pitted, and diced

Finely grated zest and juice of 1 LIME

½ cup COCONUT BUTTER, such as Nutiva brand Coconut Manna

1 teaspoon ground TURMERIC

1 cup (100g) ICE, plus more for serving

In a blender, combine all of the ingredients with 1 cup (240ml) of water and blend until smooth. Pour into 2 glasses over additional ice, if desired, and serve.

CALORIES 186

FAT 7.5g
sat 6.1g
mono 0.5g
poly 0.2g

PROTEIN 2g

CARBOHYDRATES 32g

FIBER 6g

CHOLESTEROL 0mg

IRON 1mg

SODIUM 7mg

POTASSIUM 415mg

CALCIUM 41mg

Mangos

RECIPES: **Coco-Mango Smoothie,** opposite **Pumpkin Seed-Chia Granola with Mango,** page 178 **Black Bean, Corn, Green Grape, and Avocado Salad,** page 188

The basics: Native to India, the mango tree is considered to be sacred there. Mangos are grown in tropical climates throughout the world, including Mexico, Ecuador, Peru, Guatemala, Brazil, Haiti, Florida, California, Hawaii, and Puerto Rico. Mangos are related to pistachios and cashews. Depending on the variety, the fruit can either be kidney shaped, round, or oval.

Seasonality: Mangos have two seasons: spring/summer and fall/winter. The seasons overlap, which means you'll always find at least one variety at the market throughout the year.

Good stuff: The smooth, luscious flesh and spicy-sweet flavor of the mango make it stand out from other fruits. Mangos are an excellent source of vitamin C and owe their intensely colored flesh to high levels of carotenoids, a type of antioxidant. Mangos also contain phenolic compounds, which provide the structure for antioxidants and help boost the body's immune system. They are also a good source of fiber.

Pick it: Look for mangos that yield just slightly to gentle pressure. The stem end should have a fruity aroma. Don't rely on the color to tell you how ripe a mango is. Depending on the variety, a ripe mango may be orange, red, yellow, or green-tinged.

Store it: Unripe mangos can be ripened at room temperature. Placing them in a paper bag will speed up the ripening process. Ripe mangos should be refrigerated and used within five days. Once sliced into, the mango will last in an airtight container in the refrigerator for a few days, or it can be frozen for a few months.

Use it: Rinse mangos just before using. Stand a mango upright (vertically) on a cutting board and using a sharp knife, slice off the "cheeks" of the mango on either side of the seed. Remove the remaining flesh around the seed with the knife. You can then slice the flesh of the mango cheeks and scoop it out with a spoon, or check out the opposite page for my surfer-style method of cutting up a mango for my Coco-Mango Smoothie.

Oranges

RECIPES: **Simply Red Fruit Salad,** page 18 **Spiced and Spiked Cranberry Cider,** page 40 **Cold Chaser Citrus Salad,** opposite **Calimyrna Figgy Jam,** page 87 **Sautéed Brussels Sprouts with Orange and Walnuts,** page 117

The basics: There are three types of oranges: sweet, loose-skinned, and bitter. Sweet oranges include navel, Valencia, and blood oranges. They are enjoyed for their delicious fruit as well as for juicing. Loose-skinned oranges are very easy to peel and have segments that come apart easily. Those varieties include mandarins, tangerines, clementines, satsumas, and Dancy oranges. If you've never had a bitter orange, such as the Seville or bergamot, it's because their flesh is much too tart to enjoy raw. But their peel is used to make marmalades, essential oils, and liqueurs such as Grand Marnier.

Seasonality: Oranges are available year-round, but they're at their peak in the winter, from December through March.

Good stuff: Known as a go-to source for vitamin C, one orange has all you need for the day. They're also very waist friendly, thanks to a slim 69 calories per fruit and a healthy 3g of fiber.

Pick it: Choose oranges that are firm and heavy for their size. The color on the skin should be uniform and free of dark or soft spots.

Store it: Oranges will keep in the refrigerator for up to two weeks.

Use it: Rinse the skins of oranges before using them, especially if you plan to use the zest. They're wonderful as a refreshing, fiber-rich snack, and the sections are a bright addition to salads. Orange pairs well with poultry, beef, and seafood. Orange juice adds a sweet-tart layer to drinks, sauces, and vinaigrettes.

Cold Chaser Citrus Salad

SERVES 4

Ah, the winter sniffles. They are inescapable, but you can try to ward them off with plenty of sleep, hydration, and this zingy salad. It packs 160 percent of your daily vitamin C, plus the ginger helps soothe an upset stomach.

2 PINK GRAPEFRUITS

2 NAVEL ORANGES

1 teaspoon freshly grated GINGER

¼ cup (38g) chopped CRYSTALLIZED GINGER

1. Over a bowl, using a sharp paring knife, remove the skin and white pith from the grapefruits and oranges, collecting any juices in the bowl. For each fruit, use the knife to slice alongside both membranes of each segment, releasing the citrus segments and letting them fall gently into the bowl. Squeeze the juice from the remaining membranes into a separate small bowl.

2. To the reserved juice, add the grated and crystallized ginger and whisk to blend. Drizzle the ginger mixture over the citrus segments.

3. Cover and refrigerate at least 30 minutes before serving.

CALORIES 111

FAT 0.27g
sat 0.04g
mono 0.04g
poly 0.06g

PROTEIN 1.7g

CARBOHYDRATES 28g

FIBER 3g

CHOLESTEROL 0mg

IRON 0.5mg

SODIUM 3mg

POTASSIUM 349mg

CALCIUM 60mg

Nectarine Salad with Fresh Ricotta and Pistachios

SERVES 4

Kids aren't the only ones who have trouble eating their greens. Husbands can be lukewarm on lettuce, too. Jon is willing to dive into a bowl of salad only if I've included some goodies, like nuts, fruit, or other tasty bits. And of course, whether you're trying to appeal to little ones or grown-ups, it's essential to dress your greens with a delicious dressing. Don't be afraid of the oil—a little fat is key to absorbing the fat-soluble vitamins in your veggies. The salad is shown on page 6.

2 tablespoons extra-virgin OLIVE OIL

1 tablespoon CIDER VINEGAR

2 tablespoons PEACH or APRICOT NECTAR

¼ teaspoon SALT

¼ teaspoon freshly ground BLACK PEPPER

6 cups (400g) MESCLUN GREENS

¼ cup (12g) fresh BASIL leaves

1 large ripe NECTARINE, pitted and cut into 12 slices

½ cup (about 4½ ounces/120g) RICOTTA CHEESE (see Note)

¼ cup (28g) shelled UNSALTED PISTACHIOS

1. In a small bowl, whisk together the oil, vinegar, peach or apricot nectar, salt, and pepper. Set aside.

2. Onto each of 4 salad plates, place 1½ cups (100g) of the greens, 3 nectarine slices, 2 tablespoons of the ricotta, and 1 tablespoon of the basil leaves. Drizzle each salad with 1¼ tablespoons of the vinaigrette, sprinkle with 1 tablespoon of pistachios, and serve.

NOTE: The type of ricotta cheese that is sold in the dairy section of your grocery store will work for this recipe, but I recommend you look for fresh ricotta at the cheese counter or at your farmer's market. Fresh ricotta is creamier and has a richer flavor than commercially produced cheese.

CALORIES 195

FAT 14.7g
sat 4g
mono 8g
poly 2.2g

PROTEIN 7g

CARBOHYDRATES 12g

FIBER 4g

CHOLESTEROL 16mg

IRON 1.4mg

SODIUM 202mg

POTASSIUM 205mg

CALCIUM 81mg

Apricots

RECIPES: **Apricot-Almond Clafoutis,** page 80 **Mohonk Mountain Muesli,** page 180

The basics: Spanish explorers introduced this diminutive fruit—a native of China—to the New World. Apricot trees took root in California in Spanish-missionary times and have been growing there ever since. Apricots are a drupe fruit, more commonly known as a stone fruit.

Seasonality: Apricots are in season for a painfully short time, from May through July, with their peak month being June.

Good stuff: They are a fantastic source of the antioxidant beta-carotene, which is the precursor to vitamin A and is important for a healthy immune system and eye health. Dried apricots are a great source of iron.

Pick it: Look for plump apricots that feel medium-firm when gently pressed.

Store it: Apricots are very perishable and should be enjoyed within a few days of purchase. If they're unripe, store them in a bowl at room temperature. If they're ripe, place them in a plastic bag in the refrigerator for three to five days.

Use it: Absolutely delicious as a snack, apricots also make flavorful desserts and are a natural pairing with almonds and raspberries. The golden fruits can be made into jams, chutneys, and compotes. They work in all recipes that call for peaches or plums.

What's So Great About Beta-carotene?

Beta-carotene is a vitamin that's found in plant food sources, including apricots, carrots, cantaloupe, kale, mangos, papayas, spinach, and sweet potatoes. Beta-carotene is a precursor to vitamin A, which means that it can be converted to vitamin A in the body. Vitamin A is needed for skin and eye cell growth, and it's vital for a healthy immune and reproductive system. Preformed vitamin A is only found in animal sources including dairy, fish, and meat, so beta-carotene is an important source of vitamin A for vegetarians and vegans. Vitamin A is a fat-soluble vitamin, so you need to eat a little fat to absorb it. Enjoy fresh apricots over yogurt or dried, chopped apricots mixed with nuts. Need another reason to eat more carotenoid-rich fruits and vegetables? A recent study found that just three more servings a day can measurably improve your skin's appearance, removing redness and promoting a healthier glow. Pass the papaya!

Cantaloupe

RECIPES: **Triple Melon Granita,** page 44 **Golden Gazpacho with Rock Shrimp,** page 67

The basics: The fruit we know as cantaloupe is actually a muskmelon. True cantaloupes are only grown in Europe and are not exported.

Seasonality: Cantaloupes are in season from May through September.

Good stuff: This fragrant and luscious melon is also a wonderful source of beta-carotene, the precursor to vitamin A, which is important for eye health (see sidebar, page 63). Cantaloupe is also packed with potassium, so it makes a fantastic post-workout treat.

Pick it: Choose a cantaloupe that feels heavy for its size. It should have a raised netting and a fresh, melony fragrance. The stem end should not be jagged—this means the fruit was picked too early. Avoid melons with soft spots or a very strong smell.

Store it: Unripe melons should be kept at room temperature. Once ripe, store the melons in the refrigerator. Cut melons should be wrapped tightly in plastic, refrigerated, and used within a few days.

Use it: Rinse the cantaloupe's rind before slicing into it. Scoop out the seeds with a spoon and then slice it up, or remove the flesh from the rind and cube it. A ripe cantaloupe is incredibly sweet, and a slice makes a wonderful foil to salty meats, cheeses, and olives. When cubed, the melon is a great addition to fruit salads or green salads. It adds extra refreshment to smoothies and gazpacho and is delicious in frozen desserts.

Peperonata Bruschetta

SERVES 15

Cooked bell peppers used to be on my "no" list. It didn't matter how healthy they were—I just didn't like the flavor. But peperonata, the sweet, silky pepper preparation, changed my mind. These pepper-topped toasts make a fantastic appetizer served with beer, or you can serve the peppers and onions as a side dish for chicken or steak.

4 tablespoons (60ml) OLIVE OIL

1 large ORANGE BELL PEPPER, seeded and cut into 1-inch (2.5cm) pieces

1 large YELLOW BELL PEPPER, seeded and cut into 1-inch (2.5cm) pieces

2 VIDALIA ONIONS, chopped

2 tablespoons APPLE CIDER VINEGAR

4 to 5 sprigs fresh THYME

¼ teaspoon SALT

1 BAGUETTE, preferably whole-wheat, cut crosswise into ½-inch (1.25cm) slices

1. Heat 3 tablespoons of the oil in a large sauté pan over medium heat. Add the peppers and onions and cook for about 45 minutes, stirring occasionally, until the peppers and onions are very tender. Stir in the vinegar and remove from the heat.

2. Preheat the oven to 350ºF (177ºC). Brush the baguette slices with the remaining 1 tablespoon oil. Place the baguette slices on a baking sheet and toast them in the oven for about 10 minutes, until golden. Serve the peperonata in a bowl with the toasted baguette slices alongside.

(per 2 bruschetta)

CALORIES 119

FAT 3.8g
sat 0.6g
mono 2.7g
poly 0.5g

PROTEIN 4g

CARBOHYDRATES 19g

FIBER 1g

CHOLESTEROL 0mg

IRON 1mg

SODIUM 210mg

POTASSIUM 74mg

CALCIUM 8mg

Golden Gazpacho with Rock Shrimp

SERVES 5

One of the quintessential flavors of summer is a chilled bowl of gazpacho. I make it every year, and I always try to put a new spin on it. I really like using the melon for added refreshment and smoothness. The rock shrimp bring a briny note to the table. Serve this with crusty bread, a crisp white wine, and extra-virgin olive oil for drizzling.

1 pound (450g) YELLOW or ORANGE TOMATOES, preferably heirloom varieties, diced

1 YELLOW or ORANGE BELL PEPPER, seeded and diced

½ pound (225g) CUCUMBERS, seeded and diced

1 cup (160g) cubed GOLDEN HONEYDEW or CANTALOUPE MELON

¼ diced (35g) RED ONION

1 teaspoon plus 1 tablespoon extra-virgin OLIVE OIL, plus more for serving

¼ teaspoon SALT, plus more as needed

¼ teaspoon freshly ground BLACK PEPPER, plus more as needed

1 tablespoon RED WINE VINEGAR

¼ teaspoon CHILI POWDER

1 cup (250ml) TOMATO JUICE

1 tablespoon extra-virgin OLIVE OIL, plus more for drizzling on soup

2 cloves GARLIC, minced

1 pound (450g) ROCK SHRIMP, rinsed and drained

½ AVOCADO, pitted, peeled, and diced

CRUSTY BREAD, for serving

1. Reserve one-quarter each of the diced tomatoes, bell pepper, and cucumbers for garnish; refrigerate.

2. Using a blender (or an immersion blender), pulse the remaining tomatoes, bell pepper, and cucumbers with the melon, onion, 1 teaspoon of the oil, the salt, black pepper, vinegar, and chili powder until soupy, but not entirely smooth. Add the tomato juice and blend again. Taste for seasoning and adjust, if necessary. Cover and refrigerate for at least 1 hour.

3. To serve, heat the remaining 1 tablespoon oil in a large sauté pan over high heat. Add the garlic and sauté for 1 minute. Reduce the heat to medium-high and add the shrimp to the pan. Cook the shrimp for 5 minutes, until opaque. Transfer to a plate.

4. Ladle 1 cup (250ml) of the chilled gazpacho into each of 5 bowls. Top each serving with a bit of the reserved vegetables, a few shrimp, and about 1 tablespoon of avocado. Serve with crusty bread and more olive oil for drizzling on top.

OPPOSITE: *It takes just minutes to transform this rainbow of bright ingredients into a refreshing soup.*

CALORIES 209

FAT 9.8g
sat 1.4g
mono 6.4g
poly 1.1g

PROTEIN 16g

CARBOHYDRATES 16g

FIBER 4g

CHOLESTEROL 114mg

IRON 1.4mg

SODIUM 766mg

POTASSIUM 691mg

CALCIUM 79mg

Roasted Butternut Squash Soup

SERVES 6

Naturally sweet, butternut squash makes a velvety and comforting soup for those nippy fall nights. Low in calories, rich in fiber and beta-carotene, it's also excellent for helping to boost your immune system during the winter months. To save time, you can roast the squash a day in advance.

1 (2- to 3-pound/900g to 1.3kg) BUTTERNUT SQUASH, peeled, seeded, and cut into 1-inch (2.5cm) cubes

2 tablespoons extra-virgin OLIVE OIL

¼ teaspoon SALT

¼ teaspoon freshly ground BLACK PEPPER

1 small YELLOW ONION, diced

2 sprigs fresh THYME

1 (32-ounce/1L) container low-sodium VEGETABLE BROTH

2 tablespoons CRÈME FRAÎCHE, plus more for serving

¼ teaspoon ground CINNAMON

1. Preheat the oven to 400ºF (205ºC). Place the squash in a 9-by-13-inch (23-by-33cm) baking dish, drizzle with 1 tablespoon of the oil, and season with the salt and pepper. Roast for 40 minutes, until fork tender.

2. Meanwhile, heat the remaining 1 tablespoon oil in a large sauté pan and sauté the onion with the thyme for 5 minutes. Remove from the heat and set aside; discard the thyme sprigs.

3. Remove the squash from the oven and carefully transfer it to a blender or food processor. (If using a blender, remove the center of the lid to allow steam to escape and cover the hole with a towel to prevent splashing.) Blend the squash with the sautéed onion, vegetable broth, crème fraîche, and cinnamon until smooth. Pour the soup into the sauté pan and heat through.

4. To serve, ladle a generous 1-cup (240ml) portion of the hot soup into each of 6 bowls. Top each serving with a teaspoon of crème fraîche, if desired.

CALORIES 117

FAT 5.6g
sat 1.3g
mono 3.3g
poly 0.7g

PROTEIN 1.5g

CARBOHYDRATES 17g

FIBER 5g

CHOLESTEROL 3mg

IRON 1mg

SODIUM 521mg

POTASSIUM 385mg

CALCIUM 74mg

Butternut Squash

RECIPES: **Roasted Butternut Squash Soup,** opposite **Farro Risotto with Butternut Squash and Sausage,** page 77

The basics: This elongated bell-shaped winter squash has a thick beige skin that hides the deliciously sweet orange flesh inside.

Seasonality: Butternut squash is harvested from mid-August through November. You may find it at other times of year, but it will be coming from storage, not from the field.

Good stuff: The intensely orange flesh of the butternut squash is a giveaway that it's packed with sight-saving beta-carotene. It's also a mighty source of fiber, with 1 cup (205g) of cooked squash containing one-fourth of the fiber you need for the day. And it's heart healthy, too—that 1 cup has as much potassium (important for maintaining healthy blood pressure) as a potato.

Pick it: Look for a firm squash that is heavy for its size. The skin should not have any cracks in it.

Store it: Keep butternut squash in a cool, dark place for up to a month. The thick skin helps protect it and keeps it fresh longer. Once you cut it open, the squash will keep in an airtight container in the refrigerator for up to five days.

Use it: Some people are intimidated by whole butternut squash and other winter squashes. They are tough to cut into, but a few steps should make it easier:

1. Wash the outside with warm running water.

2. Place the squash on a cutting board and slice off the very bottom end with a sharp chef's knife to make a flat surface to rest it on. Now you can use a vegetable peeler (a good one; a cheap one may break) to remove the skin, peeling in a downward motion. This wastes less squash than simply slicing off the outer skin with a knife, but you can also do that.

3. Next, slice the squash in half lengthwise and scoop out the seeds. You can either discard them, or rinse and save them for roasting. You can now cut the squash into cubes, slices, or whatever your recipe calls for.

Roasting is my favorite way to cook this vegetable. The sugars caramelize and the incredibly tasty result works well with pasta and grains, or in soups and stews. You can also steam and purée the squash. It's excellent in desserts, too—try using 1 cup (205g) of mashed butternut squash in your next batch of muffins. Its moistness will enable you to reduce the oil or butter in the recipe by half.

Sweet Potatoes

RECIPES: **Sweet Potato Moons with Balsamic Reduction,** opposite **Roasted Eggplant and Sweet Potato Dip,** page 74

The basics: Like the pumpkin, sweet potatoes were grown and used by Native Americans long before Columbus landed on New World soil. By the sixteenth century they were being cultivated in what is now the southern United States, which is why so many wonderful sweet potato recipes hail from that part of the country. Confusion still remains regarding the difference between sweet potatoes and yams. While often sold as yams, the root vegetable you're buying is probably a sweet potato. Yams are starchy tubers with brown skin and creamy flesh and are imported from the Caribbean.

Seasonality: Sweet potatoes are grown year-round in the United States.

Good stuff: Satisfying, with a rich caramel flavor, sweet potatoes are incredibly versatile. One medium baked sweet potato with skin has just 103 calories, 4g of fiber, and four times the recommended daily intake of beta-carotene, a precursor of vitamin A (see sidebar, page 63). Plus, these golden beauties offer 35 percent of your vitamin C for the day, as well as manganese, a mineral that helps keep your blood sugar level steady. Make sure to give those potatoes a drizzle of olive oil before cooking them: Vitamin A is fat soluble, so you need a little fat to absorb it.

Pick it: Sweet potatoes should be firm, with no signs of mold. They can vary wildly in size; if baking them whole, be sure to select ones of similar size so that they'll have the same cooking time.

Store it: When stored in the refrigerator, sweet potatoes can develop a hard spot in the middle. It's better to keep them in a cool, dry place with air circulating around them. They should last for two weeks.

Use it: Rinse sweet potatoes well before using them. If you're going to bake them, make sure to scrub them well with a produce brush so you can eat the crispy skin. Bake sweet potatoes at 400°F (205°C) for 40 to 50 minutes, until tender. You can also cube them, slice them, or cut them into sticks or wedges before baking, grilling, boiling, or microwaving them. Sweet potatoes work well in both sweet and savory dishes. You can use 1 cup (200g) of cooked, mashed sweet potato to replace half of the oil or butter in muffin and quick bread recipes.

Sweet Potato Moons with Balsamic Reduction

SERVES 6

I once read that if you ever find yourself on a deserted island, the sweet potato is the one food you could solely survive on. I'm not sure that's true, and I'm clearly not going to test the theory, but sweet potatoes certainly are a nutrient powerhouse. They're also a crowd-pleaser, especially with a velvety drizzle of balsamic vinegar on top.

2 to 3 pounds (900g to 1.3kg) SWEET POTATOES, peeled, halved lengthwise, and sliced into ½-inch (1.25cm) half-moons

1½ tablespoons extra-virgin OLIVE OIL

½ teaspoon KOSHER SALT

¼ teaspoon freshly ground BLACK PEPPER

½ cup (125ml) BALSAMIC VINEGAR

1. Preheat the oven to 400°F (205°C).

2. Place the sweet potatoes on a large, rimmed baking sheet in one layer and drizzle them with the oil. Sprinkle them with the salt and pepper. Bake for 40 minutes, until tender, turning once during cooking.

3. Bring the vinegar to a boil in a small saucepan. Boil until reduced to 2½ tablespoons, about 4 minutes.

4. Arrange the sweet potatoes on a large platter, drizzle them with the balsamic reduction, and serve.

CALORIES 244

FAT 3.6g
sat 0.5g
mono 2.5g
poly 0.5g

PROTEIN 4g

CARBOHYDRATES 49g

FIBER 7g

CHOLESTEROL 0mg

IRON 1.6mg

SODIUM 290mg

POTASSIUM 790mg

CALCIUM 74mg

Giardiniera (Pickled Vegetables)

MAKES ABOUT 8 CUPS (615G); SERVES 16

I've always been attracted to the large jars of giardiniera that seem to be in every Italian market in New York. And I love having the salty, tangy vegetables to munch on while I make dinner. Since I don't have an Italian grandmother to teach me how to make *sotto aceti* (under vinegar), I had to figure it out on my own, and I found that it's really not that hard. This recipe makes enough to keep you in pickled veggies for a couple of weeks.

3 cups (750ml) WHITE VINEGAR

2 tablespoons light AGAVE NECTAR

1 BAY LEAF

½ teaspoon CELERY SEEDS

½ teaspoon FENNEL SEEDS

2 tablespoons KOSHER SALT

1 head CAULIFLOWER, cut into small florets

3 CARROTS, peeled and sliced into coins

½ large ORANGE BELL PEPPER, seeded and cut into 1-inch (2.5-cm) pieces

1. In a large stockpot, bring 3 cups of water to a boil with the vinegar, agave, bay leaf, celery seeds, fennel seeds, and salt.

2. Once the brine is boiling, add the vegetables and bring back to a boil. Remove from the heat and allow the vegetables and brine to cool to room temperature.

3. Strain the mixture through a fine-mesh sieve, collecting the liquid in a container below. Discard the bay leaf and transfer the pickled vegetables to 3 pint-size (500ml) sterilized glass jars with tightly fitting lids. Pour the reserved vinegar mixture over the vegetables. If the liquid doesn't reach the top of the jars, add a little extra water or vinegar. The pickled vegetables will keep in the refrigerator for up to 2 weeks.

CALORIES 30

FAT 0.2g
sat 0.03g
mono 0.02g
poly 0.2g

PROTEIN 1g

CARBOHYDRATES 5g

FIBER 1g

CHOLESTEROL 0mg

IRON 0.3mg

SODIUM 379mg

POTASSIUM 167mg

CALCIUM 16mg

Roasted Eggplant and Sweet Potato Dip

SERVES 8

I love baba ganoush, but the color? Not so much. Eggplants have a gorgeous exterior, but once you cook them, the interior becomes a grayish mush. So I decided to perk them up with the terra–cotta tint of sweet potatoes. Serve this creamy dip with baked pita chips and fresh crudités. It's also great as a condiment on sandwiches instead of mayo.

1 medium EGGPLANT, halved lengthwise

1 large or 2 small SWEET POTATOES, halved lengthwise

3 tablespoons OLIVE OIL

¾ teaspoon SALT

¼ teaspoon freshly ground BLACK PEPPER

1 teaspoon fresh THYME leaves

¾ teaspoon CURRY POWDER

Juice of ½ LEMON

1. Preheat the oven to 425ºF (218ºC). Place the eggplant and sweet potato halves on a large, rimmed baking sheet, cut sides up, and drizzle with 2 tablespoons of the oil. Bake for 30 to 35 minutes, until completely tender. Let cool, then scoop the flesh out of the eggplant and sweet potatoes and transfer to the bowl of a food processor.

2. Add the remaining ingredients to the food processor and process until creamy. Serve immediately or transfer to an airtight container and refrigerate for up to 4 days.

CALORIES 109

FAT 5.4g
sat 0.8g
mono 3.7g
poly 0.8g

PROTEIN 1.5g

CARBOHYDRATES 15g

FIBER 4g

CHOLESTEROL 0mg

IRON 0.6mg

SODIUM 250mg

POTASSIUM 329mg

CALCIUM 24mg

Peaches

RECIPES: **White Summer Fruit Sangria,** page 47 **Berry-Nectarine Trifle,** page 52

The basics: Native to China, peaches made their way to the United States via Persia. Peaches can be golden in color with red accents or white with pink markings. All varieties have soft fuzz that covers the skin.

Seasonality: Peach season runs from May through October.

Good stuff: In addition to satisfying your sweet tooth for under 70 calories, peaches may also help prevent metabolic syndrome, which is a cluster of conditions that raise the risk of heart disease, stroke, and diabetes. A recent study found that stone fruits, including peaches, contain compounds that work to combat the syndrome. These compounds include anthocyanins, clorogenic acid, quercetin, and catechins.

Pick it: Look for very fragrant fruit that gives slightly when pressed gently. Avoid peaches with soft spots and bruises.

Store it: Keep unripe peaches and other stone fruit at room temperature until ripe. Once ripe, refrigerate for up to five days.

Use it: A ripe, juicy, sweet-smelling peach is a thing to cherish. I like to eat them right over the sink while no one is looking! Peaches are delicious raw in fruit and green salads and are also fantastic grilled and roasted. Peaches are also wonderful in drinks such as Bellinis. To remove the fuzzy exterior, blanch peaches for 30 seconds in boiling water and then place them in an ice bath. The skins will slip off easily.

Pumpkins

RECIPES: **Spice Girl Pumpkin Muffins,** page 56 **Pumpkin Seed-Chia Granola with Mango,** page 178

The basics: A member of the gourd family, the pumpkin was used by Native Americans since before the first Thanksgiving. The type of pumpkin that will yield a scary jack-o-lantern is not only bigger than what you'd want to use in the kitchen, it also contains a ton more moisture and is much more fibrous. Cooking pumpkins are fleshier and denser, which makes for a great pie, but not for decorating your front porch.

Seasonality: Pumpkins are available from September through November; availability peaks in October.

Good stuff: Pumpkin is wonderful for adding moisture to baked goods, and of course it's insanely rich in beta-carotene and fiber, and low in calories—only 49 per cup (244g) of cooked pumpkin. Pumpkin seeds, or "pepitas," are a rich source of magnesium, an important bone-building mineral.

Pick it: Look for a pumpkin that still has its stem attached. The stem should be dark green, which indicates that the pumpkin has been freshly harvested. The stem of the pumpkin is also called the "handle," but you should actually never use it to pick up the pumpkin. The color of the skin should be uniform, with no green areas. And check for soft spots—those could mean that the pumpkin was stored in a moist area and could get moldy quickly.

Store it: You can keep a whole pumpkin for up to a month at room temperature and in the refrigerator for up to three months.

Use it: Make sure to wash the surface of the pumpkin well with warm running water before using it. Cutting through the pumpkin is tough work (use a serrated knife), but once you've managed that, it's pretty smooth sailing. Scoop out the seeds (save them for roasting later) and remove any stringy bits. To make pumpkin purée, you can roast (my preferred method), steam, or even microwave the pumpkin halves and then scoop out the flesh. Then use an immersion blender (or food processor) to turn the cooked pumpkin into purée. Pumpkin purée can be used in pies, muffins, cookies, soups, sauces, or as a filling for ravioli. Roasted cubed pumpkin can be tossed with pasta and grains or used in salads. To cube the pumpkin flesh, seed the pumpkin, then peel off the thick skin and cut the flesh into cubes.

Farro Risotto with Butternut Squash and Sausage

SERVES 8

The ancient grain farro (also known as emmer) has become a culinary darling. It has a nutty flavor and chewy texture and lends itself to hearty dishes like this risotto.

1 (32-ounce/1L) container low-sodium CHICKEN or VEGETABLE BROTH

¼ cup (60ml) RED WINE

½ teaspoon SAFFRON THREADS

¼ cup (60ml) plus 1 tablespoon extra-virgin OLIVE OIL

½ YELLOW ONION, diced

1 clove GARLIC, minced

1¾ cups (350g) uncooked FARRO, rinsed

3 hot ITALIAN TURKEY SAUSAGES, casings removed

2 pounds (900g) BUTTERNUT SQUASH, peeled and diced into ¼-inch (6mm) pieces

¼ teaspoon SALT

¼ teaspoon freshly ground BLACK PEPPER

Leaves of 5 sprigs fresh THYME

⅓ cup (35g) grated PARMESAN

1. In a medium saucepan, combine 3½ cups (825ml) of the broth, the wine, and the saffron. Bring to a boil, then reduce the heat to keep the mixture at a simmer.

2. In a 2-quart (2L) saucepan over medium heat, heat ¼ cup (60ml) of the oil. Add the onion and garlic, and sauté until the onion is translucent, about 5 minutes. Add the farro and stir to coat with the oil. Cook for 3 minutes, stirring occasionally.

3. Using a ½ cup (125ml) measure or ladle, add the hot broth mixture to the farro, stirring occasionally. Allow each addition to be absorbed, 5 to 7 minutes, before adding more broth.

4. In a large sauté pan, heat the remaining 1 tablespoon oil over high heat. Add the sausage and cook, using a spatula to break it up into small pieces, for 10 minutes, until completely browned. Using a slotted spoon, transfer the sausage to a plate; leave the drippings in the pan.

5. Return the sauté pan to medium-high heat and add the squash. Season with the salt and pepper and cook, stirring occasionally, for 6 minutes. Add the remaining ½ cup (125ml) broth and cook for 12 to 15 minutes more, until tender. Set aside.

6. Add the remaining broth to the farro, the reserved squash, and the sausage, plus the thyme leaves. Cook for 5 minutes, until heated through. Sprinkle with the Parmesan before serving.

CALORIES 363

FAT 17g
sat 2.2g
mono 7.5g
poly 1.6g

PROTEIN 15g

CARBOHYDRATES 43g

FIBER 6g

CHOLESTEROL 22mg

IRON 3mg

SODIUM 663mg

POTASSIUM 418mg

CALCIUM 125mg

Red Lentil and Quinoa Cakes with Basil Cream

SERVES 8

Quinoa is the new chicken breast. It's a quick, low-fat way to get more protein in your diet.

Pinch plus 1 teaspoon SALT

1 cup (175g) uncooked QUINOA, preferably sprouted

1 cup (200g) dried RED LENTILS, rinsed

1 teaspoon ground TURMERIC

1 teaspoon ground GINGER

1 teaspoon ground CUMIN

½ teaspoon ground WHITE PEPPER

2 tablespoons OLIVE OIL

2 cups (300g) chopped YELLOW ONION

3 tablespoons ALL-PURPOSE FLOUR

2 large EGGS, whisked, or 1 large EGG, and 2 large EGG WHITES

For the basil cream:

½ cup (125ml) 2% fat GREEK YOGURT

½ cup (30g) packed fresh BASIL leaves

¼ teaspoon SALT

2 tablespoons CRÈME FRAÎCHE

1. In a medium saucepan, bring 1½ cups (350ml) of water to a boil with a pinch of salt. Place the quinoa in a fine-mesh sieve and rinse. (Sprouted quinoa does not need to be rinsed before cooking.) Add the quinoa to the boiling water, cover, and cook over medium-high heat for 10 to 15 minutes, until all the water is absorbed. Remove from the heat, stir, cover again, and let steam for 5 minutes. Let cool to room temperature.

2. In a separate saucepan, combine the lentils, turmeric, ginger, cumin, pepper, remaining 1 teaspoon of salt, and 3 cups (750ml) of water and bring to a boil. Reduce the heat to medium and simmer for 20 minutes, until the lentils are cooked down to baby food consistency and all the water has been absorbed. Let cool to room temperature.

3. Heat 1 tablespoon of the oil in large sauté pan over medium-high heat. Add the onion and sauté for 5 minutes, until translucent. Transfer to a large bowl and let cool. Wipe the pan clean and set aside.

4. Make the basil cream: Combine all the ingredients in a blender or food processor and blend until creamy.

5. When the quinoa and lentils are cool, combine them in a large bowl and add the sautéed onion, flour, and eggs.

6. Heat the remaining 1½ tablespoons oil over medium-high heat in the reserved pan. Add the lentil mixture to the pan in ¼-cup (60ml) portions in two batches, flattening the patties slightly. Cook 5 minutes per side, until golden brown.

7. Serve 2 cakes per person topped with a tablespoon of the basil cream.

CALORIES 386

FAT 22g
sat 3.8g
mono 13.9g
poly 3.6g

PROTEIN 13g

CARBOHYDRATES 35g

FIBER 6g

CHOLESTEROL 50mg

IRON 3mg

SODIUM 452mg

POTASSIUM 431mg

CALCIUM 56mg

Apricot-Almond Clafoutis

SERVES 6

I used to be intimidated by clafoutis—it sounds so fancy and French. But it's really very easy and quick to make, and while cherries (with pits!) are the classic fruit used in this dish, you can use nearly any type of fruit. I find that semi-firm stone fruits, like apricots or peaches, seem to work best. Clafoutis makes a nice dessert, but I also like it for breakfast and brunch.

1 teaspoon plus ⅓ cup (65g) SUGAR

3 APRICOTS, pitted and quartered

¼ cup (60ml) FRAMBOISE (raspberry liqueur)

1 teaspoon ALMOND EXTRACT

3 large EGGS

⅓ cup (40g) ALL-PURPOSE FLOUR

⅛ teaspoon SALT

¼ cup (½ stick/57g) UNSALTED BUTTER, melted, plus more to butter the pie dish

1 cup (250ml) 2% MILK

1 teaspoon pure VANILLA EXTRACT

2 tablespoons sliced ALMONDS

1. Preheat the oven to 325ºF (163ºC). Butter a 9-inch (23cm) pie dish and sprinkle with 1 teaspoon of the sugar.

2. Place the apricots, cut side down, in a shallow bowl and pour the liqueur and almond extract over top. Set aside.

3. In a medium bowl, whisk together the remaining ⅓ cup (65g) sugar and the eggs. Fold in the flour and salt, and then the melted butter, milk, and vanilla.

4. Arrange the apricots in a circular pattern in the prepared pie dish and then gently pour the batter over the fruit pieces. Sprinkle the almonds evenly on top and bake for 50 to 55 minutes, until lightly golden and set. Cut into 6 wedges and serve.

CALORIES 254

FAT 12g
sat 6g
mono 4g
poly 1g

PROTEIN 6g

CARBOHYDRATES 27g

FIBER 1g

CHOLESTEROL 117mg

IRON 1mg

SODIUM 106mg

POTASSIUM 153mg

CALCIUM 73mg

Yellows

This color family is a bit tougher to categorize than the others, as it spans everything from golden beets to Meyer lemons to star fruit. But this sunny group finds common ground in its wealth of antioxidant-rich compounds, which help fight chronic diseases, including cancer and heart disease.

Maui Tropical Fruit Salad with Passion Fruit Dressing

SERVES 6

Before my husband and I got married, we were lucky enough to take a trip to Maui for a food and wine festival. We stayed at the amazing Travaasa Hana Hotel, then called the Hotel Hana Maui, and visited a truly incredible fruit farm called Ono Organic Farms. I had eaten tropical fruit before, but it tasted nothing like the sweet, highly colorful, intensely fruity gems we sampled at Ono. While you're not likely to find tropical fruit that's quite as perfect as what you'd get in Hawaii, you can certainly transport yourself to a more oasis-like day with this delicious salad.

1 ripe PASSION FRUIT, halved and pulp scooped out

Juice of ½ LIME

1 teaspoon AGAVE NECTAR (light or dark)

1 STAR FRUIT, sliced

2 yellow or green KIWI FRUITS, peeled, halved, and sliced crosswise into half-moons

1 yellow PLUOT or PLUM, pitted and diced

½ DRAGON FRUIT, preferably pink inside, peeled and cubed

½ golden PINEAPPLE, peeled, cored, and cubed

2 tablespoons flaked unsweetened COCONUT

1. In a small bowl, whisk together the passion fruit pulp, lime juice, and agave nectar. Set aside.

2. In a large serving bowl, gently toss together the remaining fruits and coconut and drizzle the passion fruit dressing over top. Serve immediately or refrigerate until ready to serve.

CALORIES 81

FAT 1.4g
sat 1g
mono 0.1g
poly 0.2g

PROTEIN 1g

CARBOHYDRATES 18g

FIBER 3g

CHOLESTEROL 0mg

IRON 0.4mg

SODIUM 3mg

POTASSIUM 222mg

CALCIUM 20mg

Star Fruit

RECIPE: **Maui Tropical Fruit Salad with Passion Fruit Dressing,** opposite

The basics: Also called carambola, the star fruit is originally from Sri Lanka and the Maluku Islands. A relative newcomer to the United States, the fruit is now grown in Florida.

Seasonality: You may be able to find it year-round, but star fruit peaks from late summer through the end of winter.

Good stuff: Ripe star fruit is juicy, sweet-tart, and fragrant. The fact that it's shaped like a star means you'll most likely get your kids to try it! One cup (108g) of sliced fruit is just 33 calories and contains the carotenoid antioxidants lutein and zeaxanthin. Both of these antioxidants are found in the eye and help to protect healthy cells from harmful waves of light and reduce the risk of age-related macular degeneration and cataracts. Our bodies don't produce lutein and zeaxanthin, so we need to eat foods rich in these nutrients.

Pick it: Star fruit ripens from lime green to yellow. Choose firm fruit that is evenly colored with no blemishes.

Store it: Keep unripe star fruit at room temperature until ripe, then transfer it to the refrigerator, where it can be stored for up to fifteen days.

Use it: Rinse the edible skin of the fruit before slicing it crosswise into star-shaped pieces. If the raised edges are discolored, trim them. Remove any seeds within the fruit. Star fruit can be eaten raw in salads or cooked briefly with seafood and vegetables. Its gorgeous shape and color make it a lovely garnish for drinks and desserts.

Figs

The basics: It is said that it was the fig, not the apple, that tempted Eve in the Garden of Eden. Like the apple, figs grow on trees, but figs are actually an inverted flower. The seeds inside are the real fruit. Figs were introduced to California in the early sixteenth century by Spanish Franciscan missionaries.

Seasonality: In the United States, most commercial fig growing is limited to California. There the harvest starts in mid-May and continues through mid-December, depending on the variety. There are hundreds of fig varieties, but the ones that grow in the United States include:

Black Mission: Purple and black skin; available fresh and dried.

Calimyrna: Pale yellow-green skin; available fresh and dried.

Kadota: Amber skin; available fresh and dried.

Brown Turkey: Light purple to black skin; available fresh.

Sierra: Light golden-green skin; available fresh.

Good stuff: Figs are packed with nutrients. A serving of 3 to 4 fresh figs is 120 calories and boasts 5g of fiber, 10 percent of the daily value of potassium, and 6 percent of the daily value of calcium. Figs have also been found to contain a high concentration of phenolic compounds, which act as antioxidants. The production of phenolic compounds is a plant's way of defending itself against disease.

Pick it: Look for fresh figs with smooth, unblemished skin and no mold. Dried figs should not be too hard when gently pressed.

Store it: Figs are ripened on the tree before being harvested, so fresh figs are quite perishable and should be used within one to two days of purchase. Keep fresh figs in the refrigerator, and wash them gently just before you eat them. Dried figs can be kept for a month in a sealed bag at room temperature or for six months to a year in an airtight container in the refrigerator.

Use it: The entire fruit can be eaten, either raw or cooked. Use fresh figs in desserts such as tarts, sliced on sandwiches, and on cheese plates. Fresh and dried figs can be used in sweet and savory dishes, and pair well with pork and poultry.

Calimyrna Figgy Jam

MAKES 1¾ CUPS (570G)

I don't like to think of myself as a hoarder of jams, but rather a collector or a connoisseur, though my husband may disagree. One of the varieties I tend to stockpile is fig jam. I adore the flavor, the little crunchy seeds—everything about it. So of course when I was blessed with a large shipment of fresh figs, I immediately set about making jam. You can use any fig variety, but Calimyrnas are particularly good; the green flesh becomes golden when cooked. This jam is delicious on toast and muffins, and makes a decadent topping for yogurt or cottage cheese.

1 teaspoon finely grated ORANGE ZEST

½ cup (125ml) fresh ORANGE JUICE

1 pound (450g) fresh CALIMYRNA FIGS (about 15 to 16), quartered

¼ cup (60ml) AGAVE NECTAR (light or dark)

2 tablespoons SUGAR

Combine all of the ingredients in a medium saucepan and bring to a boil. Reduce the heat to medium and cook, uncovered, until the mixture thickens and reduces, about 30 minutes. Store in the refrigerator in a container with a tightly fitting lid for up to 1 week.

(per 2 tablespoons)

CALORIES 38

FAT 0g
sat 0g
mono 0g
poly 0g

PROTEIN 0.2g

CARBOHYDRATES 9g

FIBER 0.6g

CHOLESTEROL 0mg

IRON 0mg

SODIUM 0mg

POTASSIUM 11mg

CALCIUM 10mg

Grilled Halloumi and Lemon Salad

Halloumi hails from Cyprus and is becoming easier to find at local grocery stores. It can be made from a combination of sheep's and goat's milk, or just sheep's milk. The texture is springy and the melting point is high, which makes it ideal for grilling and frying. I love this combination of briny cheese and tangy citrus. I prefer using organic lemons in this recipe because the entire lemon is eaten.

1 clove GARLIC

¼ teaspoon SALT

2 tablespoons fresh ROSEMARY leaves

3 tablespoons extra-virgin OLIVE OIL, plus more for the grill

2 organic LEMONS, 1 juiced (2 tablespoons) and the other sliced thinly into wheels

1 (8.8-ounce/249g) package HALLOUMI, sliced horizontally into 6 large slices

1 (14-ounce/400g) can HEARTS OF PALM, rinsed, drained, and sliced into 2-inch (5-cm) pieces

1 (15-ounce/420g) can GARBANZO BEANS, rinsed and drained

1 (5-ounce/140g) container washed BABY SPINACH

1. Preheat a grill or a grill pan to medium-high.

2. Mince the garlic with the salt and rosemary. Transfer to a small bowl and whisk in the oil and the 2 tablespoons of lemon juice.

3. Brush both sides of the *halloumi* slices with some of the rosemary-lemon dressing. Set the remainder aside.

4. When ready to grill, oil the grill or pan. Add the cheese and the lemon slices and grill for 5 minutes per side, until grill marks form and the cheese is softened.

5. In a large bowl, gently toss the hearts of palm and garbanzo beans with the spinach. Arrange the salad on a platter. Drizzle the salad with the remaining rosemary-lemon dressing and serve.

CALORIES 305

FAT 20g
sat 8.5g
mono 5.5g
poly 0.8g

PROTEIN 15g

CARBOHYDRATES 20g

FIBER 6g

CHOLESTEROL 30mg

IRON 4mg

SODIUM 720mg

POTASSIUM 289mg

CALCIUM 91mg

Golden Beets with Parsley Pesto and Fregola

SERVES 4

I adore beets. They do take an annoyingly long time to roast, but the results are so worthwhile. And once you remove that drab skin, golden beets glow with such a gorgeous deep egg yolk color. If you can't find the fregola (a small, round, toasted type of pasta), you can always use Israeli couscous.

4 medium GOLDEN BEETS, trimmed

1 cup (176g) uncooked FREGOLA

1 tablespoon extra-virgin OLIVE OIL

¼ teaspoon SALT

¼ teaspoon freshly ground BLACK PEPPER, plus more for serving

For the parsley pesto:

1 large clove GARLIC

¼ teaspoon SALT

2 cups (40g) packed fresh flat-leaf PARSLEY leaves

⅓ cup (37g) shelled UNSALTED PISTACHIOS

¼ cup (25g) grated PARMESAN

⅓ cup (80ml) extra-virgin OLIVE OIL

1. Preheat the oven to 450°F (232°C). Wrap the beets tightly in foil and place them in a pie dish or on a rimmed baking sheet. Roast for 1 hour, until the beets are tender and can be pierced easily with a knife. Let cool completely. When cool, rub the beets with a paper towel to remove the skins or peel them with a sharp paring knife, and cut into quarters.

2. Bring a medium saucepan of water to a boil. Cook the fregola in the boiling water for 12 minutes; drain. Transfer the fregola to a large bowl and stir in the oil, salt, and pepper. Set aside.

3. Make the pesto: Mince the garlic with the salt, sliding the flat side of your knife over the mixture to create a paste. Place the parsley, pistachios, and cheese in the bowl of a food processor or a heavy-duty blender (such as a Vitamix). Add the garlic paste and pulse to combine. With the processor running on low, slowly pour in the oil to combine.

4. Stir the pesto into the fregola. Divide the fregola among 4 bowls, and then top each with 4 beet quarters. Grind some black pepper on top, if desired, and serve.

CALORIES 315

FAT 20g
sat 3g
mono 13g
poly 2g

PROTEIN 8g

CARBOHYDRATES 30g

FIBER 5g

CHOLESTEROL 3mg

IRON 4mg

SODIUM 341mg

POTASSIUM 460mg

CALCIUM 136mg

Curried Chicken Salad with Cashews and Grapes

SERVES 8

This is one of those recipes that I usually make over the course of two days. It's not that it's difficult, but it's so efficient to throw the chicken into my toaster oven to cook while I'm making dinner the day before. That way it's ready to go when I want to make this delicious, super-crunchy salad the next day. I love it on toasted brown bread with a few leaves of butter lettuce.

2 pounds (900g) bone-in, skin-on CHICKEN BREASTS

½ teaspoon SALT

¼ teaspoon freshly ground BLACK PEPPER

½ cup (115g) 2% plain GREEK YOGURT

¼ cup (60g) CANOLA MAYONNAISE

1 teaspoon finely grated LEMON ZEST

1 tablespoon fresh LEMON JUICE

2 teaspoons CURRY POWDER

1 large stalk CELERY, chopped

1 cup (110g) RED GRAPES, quartered

⅓ cup (50g) roasted unsalted CASHEWS, roughly chopped

¼ cup (50g) DRIED CHERRIES or RAISINS

⅓ cup (45g) diced JICAMA

1 tablespoon fresh TARRAGON leaves, chopped (optional)

1. Preheat the oven to 400ºF (205ºC). Place the chicken, skin side up, in a baking dish, sprinkle with ¼ teaspoon of the salt and the pepper, and bake for 30 minutes, until a meat thermometer inserted into the thickest part of the thigh registers 165ºF (74ºC). Set aside to cool or cover and refrigerate to use the next day.

2. When cool enough to handle, remove the skin from the chicken and discard. Remove the meat from the bone with clean hands and chop into bite-size pieces (2½ to 3 cups/250 to 375g). Place the chopped chicken in a large bowl.

3. In a small bowl, mix the yogurt and mayonnaise together thoroughly. Add the lemon zest and juice, curry powder, and the remaining ¼ teaspoon salt; stir to combine.

4. Add the yogurt mixture to the chicken and gently fold with a spatula to combine. Add the celery, grapes, cashews, dried cherries or raisins, jicama, and tarragon, if using, and stir to combine.

5. Serve the chicken salad over a bed of mixed greens or on toasted bread.

CALORIES 254

FAT 11.5g
sat 1.6g
mono 6g
poly 2.7g

PROTEIN 27g

CARBOHYDRATES 10g

FIBER 2g

CHOLESTEROL 76mg

IRON 1mg

SODIUM 384mg

POTASSIUM 527mg

CALCIUM 29mg

Lemons

The basics: Originally from Southeast Asia, lemons now grow throughout the world and are domestically grown in California. Lemons can range in size from as small as an egg to as large as an orange. Meyer lemons are much sweeter than other lemon varieties and have a flavor somewhere between a lemon and a tangerine.

Seasonality: Lemons are available year-round. Meyer lemons are in season November through March and sometimes into April.

Good stuff: Excellent for enhancing flavor without extra calories or sodium, lemons are a staple in a healthy kitchen. In addition to containing the antioxidant vitamin C, lemons also boast health-boosting bioflavonoids. Lemon peel acts as a natural antimicrobial—just another reason to use the juiced rinds to freshen your hands after cooking.

Pick it: Choose firm lemons that are heavy for their size, with uniformly yellow rinds.

Store it: Though they're lovely to look at on the counter, lemons are best kept in the refrigerator, where they will last for two to three weeks.

Use it: Lemon juice and zest help brighten up all types of dishes and drinks. To get the most from your lemons, rinse them and let them come to room temperature before using them, then roll them firmly on the counter to release the juice inside before cutting into them. You can use a juicer or cover the cut fruit with a piece of cheesecloth and squeeze the fruit with your hand. If a recipe calls for both the juice and zest of a lemon, make sure to zest the fruit before cutting into it. Lemon can be used in everything from desserts and cocktails to salad dressings, marinades, and roasts.

What Are Bioflavonoids?

The term bioflavonoids (or flavonoids) refers to a large family of plant compounds that reduce the risk of chronic diseases, including cardiovascular disease and cancer. The bioflavonoid family includes anthocyanadins, flavanols, flavanones, flavonols, flavones, and isoflavones. And yes, there will be a test at the end of the book!

Bell Peppers

The basics: Both sweet and hot peppers are members of the *Capsicum* genus that is native to Latin America. Christopher Columbus brought them back to Spain, where they became a staple of the cuisine. Officially classified as a fruit instead of a vegetable, peppers grow in a variety of colors, including yellow, orange, red, green, purple, brown, and black. Green and red bell peppers are the same type— reds are simply ripened longer and are therefore much sweeter. Bell peppers are very mild and have juicy flesh and lots of tiny white seeds inside. I personally use yellow, red, and orange bell peppers at home, but never green. I find that they can easily overwhelm a dish and have a slightly bitter flavor. I felt vindicated when legendary chef John Ash revealed to me that he too has a no-green-pepper policy. But if you like them, by all means, use them!

Seasonality: Bell peppers are grown year-round, but you may not be able to find the entire range of colors through-out the year.

Good stuff: Sweet, versatile, and great for adding color to a range of dishes, peppers are a fantastic source of vitamin C. One cup (130g) of raw sliced bell pepper has well over a day's worth of vitamin C and plenty of vitamin A for just 29 calories. While the various bell pepper colors all have similar amounts of vitamin C, red and yellow peppers have more than five times the amount of vitamin A than green ones.

Pick it: Choose colorful peppers that are firm and shiny with no bruises or cuts to the skin. Avoid ones that are limp or shriveled.

Store it: Store bell peppers in a plastic bag in the refrigerator for up to a week.

Use it: Rinse peppers before using them. Here's an easy method to remove the seeds without getting them everywhere:

1. Slice off the cap of the pepper, including the stem.

2. Proceed to cut off the sides of the pepper until only the core and seeds remain.

3. Discard the core with the seeds attached.

Peppers can be chopped or sliced and used raw on a crudité platter or in salads. They're also wonderful sautéed, roasted, grilled, in soups, or stuffed and baked.

Tortilla Soup with Homemade Chips

SERVES 6

I love a warm, comforting soup, and this one has extra kick from the jalapeño. Because the seeds are removed from the chile, it's not too spicy, but you can use just half of it if your family likes it milder. This soup is the perfect quick way to use up extra chicken.

1 tablespoon plus 2 teaspoons OLIVE OIL

½ medium YELLOW ONION, chopped finely

¼ teaspoon plus ⅛ teaspoon CHILI POWDER

1 clove GARLIC, minced

1 small JALAPEÑO, seeded and minced

1 medium YELLOW BELL or POBLANO PEPPER, seeded and diced

¼ teaspoon SALT

¼ teaspoon freshly ground BLACK PEPPER

1 (32-ounce/1L) container low-sodium CHICKEN BROTH

1 ear CORN, cooked and kernels removed, or 1 cup (185g) thawed frozen CORN

1 cup (240g) low-sodium canned BLACK BEANS, rinsed and drained

2 tablespoons fresh LIME JUICE

5 (6-inch/15cm) CORN TORTILLAS

2 cups (250g) cooked and cubed or shredded CHICKEN

⅛ teaspoon ground CUMIN

1 medium TOMATO, seeded and chopped

½ cup (20g) fresh CILANTRO leaves

1 AVOCADO, pitted, peeled, and diced

1. Heat 1 tablespoon of the oil in a stockpot over medium-high heat, then add the onion and cook for 1 minute. Add ¼ teaspoon of the chili powder and cook another 3 to 4 minutes, until the onion is translucent. Add the garlic, jalapeño, and bell or poblano pepper and cook for 3 minutes more.

2. Add the salt, black pepper, broth, corn, beans, and lime juice. Raise the heat to high, cook for 5 minutes, then tear one of the tortillas into small pieces and add it to the soup, along with the chicken. Reduce the heat and simmer for 10 minutes.

3. Meanwhile, preheat the oven or toaster oven to 350ºF (177ºC). Place the remaining 4 tortillas on a rimmed baking sheet and brush them with the remaining 2 teaspoons olive oil. Sprinkle each with a bit of the cumin and the remaining ⅛ teaspoon chili powder. Cut each into quarters (a pizza wheel works really well) and bake for 13 minutes, until crispy and lightly golden.

4. Add the tomato and cilantro to the soup and raise the heat to medium; cook for 3 minutes. Serve hot, with the tortilla chips and avocado on the side.

CALORIES 304

FAT 12.5g
sat 2.1g
mono 6.7g
poly 1.6g

PROTEIN 22g

CARBOHYDRATES 30g

FIBER 7g

CHOLESTEROL 52mg

IRON 1.6mg

SODIUM 519mg

POTASSIUM 609mg

CALCIUM 37mg

Meyer Lemon Pound Cake

SERVES 12

Who doesn't love pound cake? Maybe there's someone out there, but I have yet to meet them. Besides being a crowd-pleaser, it's incredibly versatile. It's excellent on its own, with ice cream, and in my Berry-Nectarine Trifle (page 52), and it makes a to-die-for French toast. You might as well make two loaves while you're at it. Eat one now and freeze the other for later.

6 tablespoons (¾ stick/85g) UNSALTED BUTTER, softened, plus more for the pan

1½ cups (180g) ALL-PURPOSE FLOUR, plus more for the pan

½ teaspoon SALT

¼ teaspoon BAKING SODA

2 large EGGS

½ cup (115g) low-fat SOUR CREAM

1 teaspoon finely grated MEYER LEMON ZEST

¼ cup (60ml) fresh MEYER LEMON JUICE (from 2 lemons)

1 cup (200g) SUGAR

1. Preheat the oven to 325ºF (163ºC). Grease and flour a 9-by-5-inch (23-by-12.75cm) loaf pan. Set aside.

2. Combine the flour, salt, and baking soda in a medium bowl and set aside.

3. Whisk the eggs with the sour cream and the lemon zest and juice in a medium bowl and set aside.

4. Place the butter in a large bowl and, using an electric mixer on medium speed, beat until creamy. Scrape the sides of the bowl down and add the sugar in two additions, beating until blended after each one. Add the sour cream mixture and mix. Add half of the flour mixture and mix again. Stir in the remaining flour mixture by hand.

5. Transfer the dough to the prepared pan. Bake for 65 minutes, until lightly golden on top. Let cool in the pan.

CALORIES 202

FAT 8g
sat 4.7g
mono 1.8g
poly 0.4g

PROTEIN 3g

CARBOHYDRATES 30g

FIBER 0.5g

CHOLESTEROL 51mg

IRON 0mg

SODIUM 142mg

POTASSIUM 57mg

CALCIUM 26mg

Fig and Nectarine Crostata

SERVES 6

While I love to bake, I'm certainly not a pastry pro. That's why I like crostatas—they're not only delicious, but also forgiving since they needn't be perfectly round. I also like the fruit-to-crust ratio. And using ripe, seasonal fruit means you won't have to add much sugar.

For the dough:

½ cup (62g) WHOLE-WHEAT FLOUR

1 cup (120g) ALL-PURPOSE FLOUR

¼ teaspoon BAKING POWDER

¼ cup (50g) SUGAR

1 teaspoon finely grated LEMON ZEST

¼ teaspoon SALT

6 tablespoons (¾ stick/85g) chilled UNSALTED BUTTER, cut into small pieces

¼ cup (60ml) ICE WATER

For the filling:

½ pound (225g) fresh FIGS, sliced

2 NECTARINES, sliced thin and seeded

¼ cup (50g) SUGAR

3 teaspoons CORNSTARCH

¼ cup (30g) chopped WALNUTS

1 large EGG WHITE, beaten

1 tablespoon DEMERARA SUGAR or other coarse sugar

1. Make the dough: In a food processor, combine the whole-wheat flour, all-purpose flour, baking powder, sugar, lemon zest, and salt. Add the butter and pulse until the mixture looks like coarse meal. With the food processor running on low speed, slowly add ice water until the dough just comes together (you may not need all the water). With clean hands, gather the dough up and form it into a ball. Wrap in plastic wrap and refrigerate for 1 hour or overnight.

2. Preheat the oven to 375ºF (190ºC). Cover a rimmed baking sheet with a Silpat mat or coat with cooking spray and line with parchment paper; set aside.

3. Make the filling: In a large bowl, toss the fruit with the sugar, cornstarch, and walnuts. Set aside.

4. Remove the dough from the refrigerator and unwrap it, leaving the plastic wrap beneath the dough. Place another large sheet of plastic wrap on top of the dough. Roll the dough out into a 10-inch (25.5cm) circle; remove the plastic wrap from the top of the dough. Add the fruit mixture to the center of the dough, leaving a 3-inch (8cm) border. Fold the dough over to form an edge.

5. Using a pastry brush, coat the dough with the egg. Sprinkle the demerara sugar over the dough and exposed fruit. Bake for 40 minutes, until the crust is golden and the fruit is bubbly (some juice will escape from the crust). Display great patience while waiting 10 minutes for the crostata to cool slightly and set. Slice into wedges and serve.

CALORIES 379

FAT 15g
sat 7.6g
mono 3.9g
poly 2.5g

PROTEIN 6g

CARBOHYDRATES 57g

FIBER 4g

CHOLESTEROL 31mg

IRON 1mg

SODIUM 132mg

POTASSIUM 204mg

CALCIUM 37mg

Greens

There's a reason why there are more recipes in this chapter than any other in the book—green is Mother Nature's favorite color. She uses it to paint everything from leafy herbs to creamy avocados to refreshing cucumber. Most members of the green family are super slimming, with less than 50 calories per cup, so make friends with them and load your plate high. They also offer up mega amounts of antioxidants for longevity-boosting benefits. And many greens are a fabulous meat-free source of iron, as well as the B-vitamin folate, which is essential for a healthy pregnancy.

Mini Asparagus and Gruyère Frittatas

MAKES 12 MINI FRITTATAS

Jon and I have people over for brunch a lot. It's the easiest time to host and you nab the kids before naptime meltdown hits. Some variation of these frittatas are nearly always on the menu. When you go mini, you not only free up your hands for more important tasks, like wiping drool from your son's chin, you also end up with servings that are easy to freeze if there are leftovers. Plus, they help you practice portion control. The asparagus is tasty, but if you don't have that, you can use spinach or broccoli florets.

COOKING SPRAY, for the pan

6 large EGGS

2 large EGG WHITES

¼ teaspoon SALT

¼ teaspoon freshly ground BLACK PEPPER

½ cup (120ml) 1% MILK

½ cup (1¾ ounces/50g) shredded GRUYÈRE CHEESE

2 teaspoons fresh THYME leaves, finely chopped (optional)

1 tablespoon OLIVE OIL

1 SHALLOT, minced

¾ bunch ASPARAGUS, cut into 1-inch (2.5cm) pieces, or 2 cups (200g) other green vegetables

1. Preheat the oven to 375ºF (190ºC). Spray a 12-cup muffin pan with cooking spray.

2. In a large bowl, whisk together the eggs and egg whites. Stir in the salt, pepper, milk, cheese, and thyme, if using. Set aside.

3. In a small sauté pan, heat the oil over high heat. Add the shallot and sauté for 1 minute. Add the asparagus and sauté for 5 minutes more, until the asparagus is bright green. Allow to cool slightly, then add the shallot-asparagus mixture to the bowl with the egg mixture.

4. Evenly pour the egg mixture into the wells of the prepared pan and place it in the middle of the oven. Bake for 23 minutes, until the tops are golden and a toothpick inserted in the middle comes out clean. Allow the frittatas to cool slightly, then pop them out of the pan and serve. Or let them cool completely, remove them from the pan, and store them in an airtight container in the refrigerator for up to 3 days or in the freezer for up to 3 months. Reheat frozen frittatas in a 325ºF (163ºC) degree oven for 20 minutes.

CALORIES 79

FAT 5g
sat 1.9g
mono 2.3g
poly 0.7g

PROTEIN 6g

CARBOHYDRATES 2g

FIBER 0.6g

CHOLESTEROL 98mg

IRON 1mg

SODIUM 123mg

POTASSIUM 120mg

CALCIUM 80mg

Avocado Smoothie

SERVES 2

We're really into avocados at my house. Between me, my husband, and my son, Leo, we eat several each week. They usually get diced and tossed into salads and tacos, or smeared onto bread, but it wasn't until recently that we started to drink them. An avocado might not seem like a go-to smoothie component, but when it's blended with ingredients that are sweet, it provides body and richness. With its super-high potassium content, it's just the right thing, along with banana, to enjoy after a tough workout. If you want to make this a vegan smoothie, just omit the yogurt, or use cultured coconut or almond milk.

½ ripe AVOCADO, pitted and peeled

½ large BANANA

¼ cup (60g) low-fat VANILLA YOGURT

¼ cup ICE (about 2 cubes), plus more for serving

¾ to 1 cup (125ml) COCONUT WATER, depending on your preferred thickness

1 teaspoon AGAVE NECTAR (light or dark)

¼ teaspoon ground CINNAMON, plus more for sprinkling

Combine all of the ingredients in a blender. Blend until smooth and frothy. Sprinkle additional cinnamon on top and serve.

CALORIES 155

FAT 8g
sat 1.5g
mono 5g
poly 1g

PROTEIN 3g

CARBOHYDRATES 20g

FIBER 5g

CHOLESTEROL 1.5mg

IRON 0.6mg

SODIUM 90mg

POTASSIUM 569mg

CALCIUM 81mg

Asparagus

RECIPES: **Mini Asparagus and Gruyere Frittatas,** page 102 **Panzanella Niçoise Salad,** page 121

The basics: A member of the lily family, these stalks are originally from the Mediterranean. The most common color is green, but you'll also find white asparagus, which is grown underground and prized by Europeans, as well as a purple variety.

Seasonality: Asparagus is available from February through June.

Good stuff: Along with its distinctive flavor and shape, asparagus boasts a nice nutritional résumé. For each 40-calorie cup (180g) of cooked asparagus, you get 243 micrograms (mcg) of the B-vitamin folate. Pregnant women need 600 to 800mcg of folate daily, and this nutrient is also important for a healthy heart. Asparagus also contains plenty of sight-saving vitamin A, lutein, and zeaxanthin.

Pick it: Look for firm, bright green (unless purchasing white or purple asparagus) spears with tight buds. There should be no signs of wetness on the buds. Avoid limp spears.

Store it: Keep asparagus in a plastic bag in the refrigerator for no more than four days.

Use it: Asparagus is grown in sandy soil, so be sure to give it a thorough rinsing before using it. Asparagus spears have a natural "snapping point." If you hold the last quarter of the stalk between your thumbs and forefingers and bend it, the end will snap off. Of course, you can always simply trim off the bottom ½ inch (1.25cm) with a knife. If the stalks are thick and woody, you may want to peel the ends with a vegetable peeler. Asparagus is wonderful sautéed, roasted, stir-fried, blanched, or steamed. It's delicious in salads, omelets, and other egg dishes, or tossed with pasta.

Mustard Greens

RECIPE: **Mustard Green Frittata,** opposite

The basics: A favorite in soul food cuisine, the leaves of the mustard plant have a distinctive horseradish-pepper flavor. Mustard greens are also used in Indian and Nepalese cooking.

Seasonality: Mustard greens are in season from December through April, but can be found at other times of the year.

Good stuff: Though it's not as popular as spinach or kale, this dark, leafy green should get more attention than it does. The pungent flavor of mustard greens adds a delicious bite to dishes, and it has extraordinary health benefits. One cup (86g) of cooked mustard greens has 36 calories and is loaded with beta-carotene (a precursor to vitamin A; see sidebar, page 63), lutein, and zeaxanthin. Lutein and zeaxanthin are antioxidants that help to protect healthy eye cells and reduce the risk of age-related macular degeneration and cataracts. Mustard greens contain nine times the Adequate Intake (AI) of vitamin K, which is essential for blood clotting. Some studies show that it helps keep bones strong in the elderly. If you're taking blood-thinning medications, you should avoid mustard greens and other dark, leafy greens.

Pick it: Look for dark, crisp green leaves. Avoid mustard greens with very thick stems.

Store it: Mustard greens will keep for one week in the refrigerator, tightly wrapped in plastic.

Use it: Wash mustard greens just before using them. Remove the stems and chop the leaves. The deep, intense flavor of mustard greens makes them a great accompaniment for meat, and they go especially well with salty bacon. Mustard greens can be sautéed, braised, or blanched.

Mustard Green Frittata

SERVES 6

Mustard greens can be a tough sell. They have the intense flavor of kale and arugula, and a boatload of health benefits, but they haven't been elevated to cult status yet. It's true, the leaves are a bit tough and require some cooking time to soften, but they work nicely in this frittata, adding an addictively earthy bite.

4 teaspoons OLIVE OIL

1 medium ONION, chopped

1 bunch MUSTARD GREENS, chopped

10 large EGGS

½ cup (125ml) 2% MILK

¼ teaspoon SALT

¼ teaspoon ground RED PEPPER

⅓ cup (about 1¼ ounces/35g) grated PARMESAN

1. Preheat the oven to 350ºF (177ºC).

2. Heat 3 teaspoons of the oil in an ovenproof 10- to 12-inch (25.5- to 30.5cm) sauté pan over medium-high heat. Add the onion and cook for about 5 minutes, until translucent. Add the mustard greens and cook for 10 minutes, until wilted.

3. In a large bowl, whisk together the eggs, milk, salt, red pepper, and cheese.

4. Add the remaining 1 teaspoon oil to the pan with the mustard greens, heat briefly over high heat, then add the egg mixture. Cook for 6 minutes, until the edges are set.

5. Transfer the sauté pan to the oven and cook for 15 to 18 minutes, until the top looks dry and the egg mixture is completely set. Cut into 6 wedges and serve.

CALORIES 193

FAT 13g
sat 4g
mono 5g
poly 2g

PROTEIN 14g

CARBOHYDRATES 5g

FIBER 1g

CHOLESTEROL 316mg

IRON 2mg

SODIUM 328mg

POTASSIUM 269mg

CALCIUM 171mg

Fennel and Grapefruit Salad with Chamomile Vinaigrette

SERVES 4

When you think about relaxing after a long day, a glass of red wine probably comes to mind. But you might want to give this salad a try instead. Fennel is packed with blood-pressure regulating potassium, and chamomile has long been known to help settle nerves, and may also provide a boost to your immune system. And besides all that—it's tasty.

⅓ cup (80ml) APPLE CIDER VINEGAR

2 CHAMOMILE tea bags

2 large FENNEL bulbs (about 2 pounds, 6 ounces/1kg), trimmed, halved lengthwise, and cored, fronds reserved for garnish

1 large PINK GRAPEFRUIT

¼ cup (60ml) extra-virgin OLIVE OIL

¼ teaspoon SALT

¼ teaspoon freshly ground BLACK PEPPER

1. Warm the vinegar in a small saucepan over low heat. Add the tea bags (wrapping the strings around the pan handle) and let steep for 5 to 7 minutes; remove from the heat, discard the tea bags, and let cool.

2. Slice the fennel bulb into pieces about ⅛ inch (3mm) thick and transfer to a large serving bowl.

3. Over a bowl, using a sharp paring knife, remove the skin and white pith from the grapefruit, collecting any juices in the bowl. Use the knife to slice alongside both membranes of each segment, releasing the citrus segments and letting them fall gently into the bowl. Squeeze any remaining juice from the membranes. Using a slotted spoon, transfer the segments to a plate, leaving the juice in the bowl.

4. In the same small bowl with the grapefruit juice, add the oil, salt, and pepper. Whisk in the cooled vinegar.

5. Toss the fennel with the vinaigrette, arrange the grapefruit segments on top, garnish with the reserved fennel fronds, and serve.

CALORIES 193

FAT 14g
sat 2g
mono 10.8g
poly 1.3g

PROTEIN 2g

CARBOHYDRATES 16g

FIBER 5g

CHOLESTEROL 0mg

IRON 1mg

SODIUM 237mg

POTASSIUM 616mg

CALCIUM 69mg

Fennel

RECIPE: **Fennel and Grapefruit Salad with Chamomile Vinaigrette,** opposite

The basics: There are actually two types of fennel. One is a leafy herb that produces fennel seeds, called common fennel, and the other is the bulbous Florence fennel, which is used as a vegetable and is also referred to as "sweet fennel." From here on out, I'll refer to Florence fennel simply as "fennel."

Seasonality: Fennel grows year-round in the United States.

Good stuff: It has a wonderful, light licorice flavor and a great crunch. It's super low in calories—1 cup (107g) raw has just 27. It's rich in heart-healthy potassium and is a fairly good non-dairy source of calcium.

Pick it: Look for fennel bulbs without any bruises or brown spots. The fronds, if attached, should be bright green and feathery.

Store it: Keep fennel in a plastic bag in the refrigerator for up to five days.

Use it: The entire fennel plant is edible. For simple snacking or using in salads, remove the stalks, slice the bulb in half lengthwise, and remove the core. Cut the fennel into chunks and use raw as a crudité in addition to carrots and celery. The fronds—as long as they are fresh and undamaged—can be used as you would use dill or parsley. Just chop them up and add a bit to a dish before serving. They can also be used in cooking soups made with the fennel bulb. The fennel bulb and stalks can also be roasted, grilled, or braised.

Kale

RECIPE: **Kale Salad with Watermelon Radishes,** opposite

The basics: A member of the cabbage family, kale grows in several varieties and colors. The leaves do not form a head, can be either curly or smooth, and range in color from dark green to purple to green tinged with purple.

Seasonality: Kale is available year-round, but peaks in the winter.

Good stuff: Packed with beta-carotene and sight-saving lutein and zeaxanthin, this dark, leafy green is easy on the eyes. With 472mcg per 1-cup (67g) serving, kale is one of the richest sources of vitamin K, which is important for blood clotting. (Kale intake should be limited if you're taking blood-thinning medication.) It's also quite slimming at 33 calories per serving.

Pick it: Choose kale with deeply colored leaves that show no signs of wilting or discoloration.

Store it: Keep kale in the refrigerator for no longer than two to three days. If you place a damp paper towel around the stem ends and place it in a plastic bag, it will remain crisp.

Use it: Wash kale just before using it and remove the fibrous center stalks. Kale can be eaten raw, but the smooth varieties make for tastier salads. Kale can also be sautéed, braised, added to soups and stews, or baked into chips.

Kale Salad with Watermelon Radishes

SERVES 4

Raw kale salads have become as ubiquitous on restaurant menus as locally made cheeses, but many of them feel like a plateful of hay on the palate. I wanted to create one that tasted really fresh, but didn't make me feel like I was choking down a bunch of roughage. The key is using the right kale. Avoid curly varieties and be sure to remove all of the tough stems. Also, kale is best when it's super-fresh, and since this recipe is so simple, there's no reason to let it languish in the fridge for a week. The salad is shown on the front cover.

1 teaspoon finely grated LEMON ZEST

2 tablespoons fresh LEMON JUICE

2 tablespoons extra-virgin OLIVE OIL

¼ teaspoon SALT

¼ teaspoon freshly ground BLACK PEPPER

1 bunch KALE, preferably Even' Star or lacinato (Toscano or "dinosaur") variety, stems removed and leaves sliced into ribbons

3 small WATERMELON RADISHES, trimmed and sliced into rounds

⅓ cup (50g) unsalted CASHEWS, toasted (see Note)

⅓ cup (50g) GOLDEN RAISINS

1. In a small bowl, whisk together the lemon zest and juice, oil, salt, and pepper. Set the dressing aside.

2. In a large serving bowl, toss the kale with the radishes. When ready to serve, toss with the dressing and garnish with the cashews and raisins. Serve.

NOTE: To toast the cashews, heat them in a dry pan over medium-high heat until fragrant, 4 to 5 minutes, shaking the pan occasionally, and being careful not to let the nuts burn.

CALORIES 212

FAT 13g
sat 2g
mono 9g
poly 2g

PROTEIN 4g

CARBOHYDRATES 23g

FIBER 3g

CHOLESTEROL 0mg

IRON 2mg

SODIUM 203mg

POTASSIUM 490mg

CALCIUM 95mg

Green Apple–Watercress Salad with Buttermilk Dressing

SERVES 6

My friend Jo, like many Brits, is wild about watercress. I suppose that's because it's used in traditional tea sandwiches. It seems Americans are warming up to the supergreen, and that's smart—studies show that it helps fight damage caused by free radicals.

2 bunches WATERCRESS, tough stems removed, chopped (8 cups)

1 large GRANNY SMITH APPLE, cored and sliced into matchsticks (1½ cups/150g)

2 stalks CELERY, cut into small dice

½ cup (125ml) low-fat BUTTERMILK

⅛ teaspoon SALT

⅛ teaspoon ground WHITE PEPPER

½ AVOCADO, pitted and peeled

1 teaspoon LEMON ZEST

1 tablespoon fresh LEMON JUICE

1 teaspoon HONEY

1. Combine the watercress, apple, and celery in a large serving bowl; set aside.

2. In a blender, combine the remaining ingredients and blend until smooth. Toss the dressing with the salad and serve immediately, or reserve the dressing in an airtight container in the refrigerator until ready to serve, up to a day (whisk before using).

CALORIES 66

FAT 2.8g
sat 0.5g
mono 1.7g
poly 0.4g

PROTEIN 2.3g

CARBOHYDRATES 10g

FIBER 2.5g

CHOLESTEROL 0.8mg

IRON 0.3mg

SODIUM 104mg

POTASSIUM 349mg

CALCIUM 90mg

Watercress

RECIPE: **Green Apple–Watercress Salad with Buttermilk Dressing,** opposite

The basics: As its name suggests, watercress is grown in running water and can be found growing wild near streams and brooks. It has small, mustard-flavored leaves and grows in bunches. It's a favorite of Brits, perhaps because British explorers used it to fend off scurvy. This member of the cruciferous family also makes a great filling for tea sandwiches.

When it's in season: Watercress is available year-round, and is primarily grown hydroponically.

Good stuff: At 4 calories per cup (34g), watercress is a girl's best friend. It's also high in isothiocyanates, which may help prevent cancer by aiding the body in getting rid of potential carcinogens.

Pick it: Watercress is sold in little bouquets. Look for bright green leaves with a fresh scent and no signs of wetness.

Store it: Refrigerate in a plastic bag for up to five days. You can also place it stem down in a vase of water.

Use it: Wash and dry gently before using. Watercress can be enjoyed raw or cooked, but keep the cooking brief. It's delicious in soups (add it at the end), with eggs, in sauces and pestos, in salads, and, of course, in sandwiches.

Brussels Sprouts

RECIPE: **Sautéed Brussels Sprouts with Orange and Walnuts,** page 117

The basics: Part of the cruciferous family, these mini cabbages grow on a large stalk. The sprouts were likely cultivated in Belgium in the sixteenth century, hence their name.

Seasonality: Brussels sprouts can be found from late August through March. They peak in the fall.

Good stuff: Contrary to what many people think, Brussels sprouts are delicious! The trick is to not overcook them. When overcooked, their cabbage-y flavor becomes too pronounced, plus they're less nutritious. Like broccoli (page 119), Brussels sprouts are loaded with anticancer properties, and they contain an even higher amount of glucosinolates. Sprouts are also rich in vitamin C, folate, and potassium.

Pick it: Look for Brussels sprouts with tightly packed green leaves without holes or discoloration. And when you pick out your sprouts, select ones with a uniform size so that they will cook evenly. Smaller sprouts are also generally tastier than big ones.

Store it: Brussels sprouts will keep in a plastic bag in the refrigerator for up to four days. Wash well just before using.

Use it: Trim the woody ends of the sprouts with a sharp knife. Remove and discard any loose leaves. They can then either be cooked whole, halved, or shredded. Roasting brings out their nuttiness, but stir-frying and steaming are also healthy cooking methods you can use.

Minted Peas with Sautéed Shrimp

SERVES 6

I'm not really sure why peas have earned a reputation as a hated vegetable. I suppose canned peas and overcooked frozen peas could create an aversion to the sweet little legumes, but as long as you cook them gently, they're incredibly delicious. If you keep frozen peas and dried penne on hand, all you need to do is pick up some shrimp for a quick weeknight meal. And if you buy shrimp that are already peeled and deveined, everything comes together even faster.

1 pound (450g) box WHOLE-WHEAT PENNE

2 cups frozen SWEET PEAS

⅛ teaspoon plus ¼ teaspoon SALT

1 teaspoon UNSALTED BUTTER

2 tablespoons chopped fresh MINT leaves

2 tablespoons grated PARMESAN

2 tablespoons extra-virgin OLIVE OIL

2 large cloves GARLIC

1 pound (450g) medium SHRIMP, peeled and deveined

⅛ teaspoon freshly ground BLACK PEPPER

1 teaspoon LEMON ZEST

1. Bring a large pot of salted water to a boil and cook the penne according to the package directions. Drain.

2. Place the peas and enough water to cover them in a small saucepan and bring to a boil. Cook for 5 minutes, then drain the peas. Combine the hot peas with ⅛ teaspoon of the salt, the butter, mint, 1 tablespoon of the cheese, and 1 tablespoon of the oil. Set aside and keep warm.

3. Meanwhile, in a large sauté pan, heat the remaining 1 tablespoon oil over medium-high heat. Grate the garlic into the pan with a Microplane grater and cook for 1 minute. Add the shrimp and season with the remaining ¼ teaspoon salt and the pepper. Cook the shrimp for about 2 minutes per side, until pink.

4. In a large serving bowl, toss the hot shrimp with the penne and peas. Sprinkle with the remaining 1 tablespoon cheese and the lemon zest, and serve.

CALORIES 403

FAT 8.6g
sat 1.5g
mono 3.6g
poly 0.8g

PROTEIN 22g

CARBOHYDRATES 59g

FIBER 8g

CHOLESTEROL 99mg

IRON 2.5mg

SODIUM 675mg

POTASSIUM 425mg

CALCIUM 104mg

Sautéed Brussels Sprouts with Orange and Walnuts

SERVES 8

People are finally warming up to Brussels sprouts, and I couldn't be happier (I have always loved them). I remember heading to the Dupont Circle farmer's market when I lived in Washington, DC, and discovering that the diminutive cabbages actually grow on branches! I was so eager to pedal home on my mountain bike (with the sprouts poking out of my basket) to cook them up. I guarantee that you will be able to convert any remaining Brussels sprout–phobes with this easy, enticing dish.

⅓ cup (30g) WALNUTS, coarsely chopped

1 NAVEL ORANGE

2 tablespoons extra-virgin OLIVE OIL

1 SHALLOT, minced

2 pounds (900g) BRUSSELS SPROUTS, trimmed and halved

¼ teaspoon SALT

¼ teaspoon freshly ground BLACK PEPPER

1. Toast the walnuts in a small dry sauté pan over medium-high heat, shaking the pan occasionally, until fragrant, 4 minutes. Set aside. Zest the entire orange and juice half of it (approximately ¼ cup/60ml). Set the zest and juice aside and reserve the other half of the orange for another use.

2. In a 12-inch (30.5cm) sauté pan, heat 1 tablespoon of the oil over medium-high heat, then add the shallot and cook for 1 minute. Add half of the Brussels sprouts, cut side down, in a single layer, and sprinkle with ⅛ teaspoon of the salt. Cook for 4 minutes, then add half of the orange juice to the pan, flip the sprouts, and cook for 4 minutes more. Transfer the sprouts to a large serving bowl.

3. Add the remaining 1 tablespoon oil to the pan and cook the second batch of sprouts as you did the first, using the remaining ⅛ teaspoon salt and remaining orange juice. Add the second batch of sprouts to the serving bowl.

4. Toss the sprouts with the reserved walnuts and orange zest and season with black pepper. Serve warm, at room temperature, or chilled as a salad.

CALORIES 119

FAT 7g
sat 0.9g
mono 3.2g
poly 2.8g

PROTEIN 5g

CARBOHYDRATES 13g

FIBER 5g

CHOLESTEROL 0mg

IRON 1.8mg

SODIUM 102mg

POTASSIUM 495mg

CALCIUM 55mg

Nutty Broccoli

SERVES 4

This is one of those veggie dishes that actually makes you want to go back for seconds. If you're using frozen broccoli, make sure it's completely thawed and drained before sautéing.

⅓ cup (35g) PECANS

2 tablespoons OLIVE OIL

1 large head BROCCOLI, cut into 1-inch (2.5cm) pieces, or 1 (16-ounce/450g) bag frozen broccoli florets (about 4 cups), thawed and drained

¼ teaspoon SALT

¼ teaspoon freshly ground BLACK PEPPER

¼ teaspoon CRUSHED RED PEPPER

1. Preheat the oven or toaster oven to 350ºF (177ºC). Place the pecans on a rimmed baking sheet and toast for about 6 minutes, until the nuts are fragrant. Allow to cool, then chop coarsely.

2. Heat the oil in a large sauté pan over high heat. Turn down to medium heat, add the broccoli, salt, and black pepper, and cook for 12 to 15 minutes, stirring occasionally. The broccoli should be tender, but still have a slight crunch. Some of it will be browned.

3. Sprinkle the crushed red pepper and chopped pecans on top, toss gently, and serve hot or at room temperature.

CALORIES 140

FAT 13g
sat 1.5g
mono 8.8g
poly 2.5g

PROTEIN 3g

CARBOHYDRATES 5g

FIBER 3g

CHOLESTEROL 0mg

IRON 0.9mg

SODIUM 194mg

POTASSIUM 269mg

CALCIUM 41mg

Broccoli

RECIPE: **Nutty Broccoli,** opposite

The basics: Part of the cruciferous family, broccoli is related to cauliflower, Brussels sprouts, bok choy, and kohlrabi.

Seasonality: Broccoli is grown year-round, but its peak season is from October through April.

Good stuff: Often touted for its anticancer benefits, broccoli is a rich source of sulfur-containing compounds called glucosinolates, which explains the smell when you overcook it. The breakdown of glucosinolates creates sulforaphane and indole-3-carbinol (I3C), both of which may help prevent the formation of cancerous cells by killing off potential carcinogens in the body. One cup (94g) of cooked broccoli has 52 calories, 5.5g of fiber, 94mg of calcium (about as much as half an ounce of cheese), and 74mg of vitamin C, which is almost as much as an orange contains.

Pick it: Look for firm broccoli heads with tight buds and no mushy or wet-looking spots.

Store it: Keep broccoli in the refrigerator in an airtight bag for up to four days. Rinse just before preparing.

Use it: Both the stems and florets of broccoli are edible and can be enjoyed raw or cooked. Remember those awesome glucosinolates? They tend to leach into cooking liquid, so avoid boiling broccoli. It's best to steam or sauté it until just cooked. Overcooking may decrease broccoli's cancer-fighting power. You can also microwave it, but keep the cooking time short.

Avocados

RECIPES: **Ultimate Breakfast Sandwich,** page 23 **Grilled Shrimp Tacos,** page 38 **Golden Gazpacho with Rock Shrimp,** page 67 **Tortilla Soup with Homemade Chips,** page 95 **Avocado Smoothie,** page 104 **Green Apple–Watercress Salad with Buttermilk Dressing,** page 112 **Corn and Basil Crab Toasts,** page 129 **Black Bean, Corn, Green Grape, and Avocado Salad,** page 188

The basics: Native to the tropics and subtropics, the avocado is the fruit of the avocado tree. The word avocado comes from *ahuacatl*, the Aztec word for testicle.

Seasonality: California avocados are in season from spring through fall. They are imported from other countries during the rest of the year.

Good stuff: The creamy texture and nutty, grassy flavor of avocados make them extremely versatile. Thanks to their nutrient density (there's a lot of good stuff packed into each serving), mashed avocados make an excellent first solid food for babies. They're rich in heart–healthy monounsaturated fat and are a surprisingly good source of fiber. Half of an avocado has 114 calories, nearly 5g of fiber, and 345mg of potassium. Avocados are also rich in lutein, an antioxidant that may play a role in keeping eyes healthy.

Pick it: A ripe avocado should be firm, but yielding if squeezed gently. A Hass avocado will turn from green to black when ripe, but other varieties remain green.

Store it: It's ideal to use ripe avocados immediately, but they can be stored in the refrigerator for a maximum of two days. Store unripe fruit at room temperature or place in a brown paper bag with an apple or banana. The ethylene gas released by apples, bananas, and tomatoes speeds the ripening process.

Use it: Rinse the skin of the fruit before slicing into it. Cut it lengthwise around the seed with a sharp knife, then rotate the two halves to separate them. Use a spoon to remove and discard the seed. You can then either slice the fruit into a crosshatch pattern and lift out the cubes with a knife or spoon, or simply scrape the fruit into a bowl with a spoon. Use the fruit cubed in salads and smoothies or mashed for dips and spreads. Avocados can also be used in desserts and can replace some of the butter without a loss of richness. Avocados do not hold up well to heat, which is why they are used raw. But you can add them as a topping on hot dishes. To prevent cut avocados from oxidizing and turning brown, sprinkle the flesh with lemon or lime juice or white vinegar.

Panzanella Niçoise Salad

SERVES 4

A *panzanella* is a bread salad. Italian in origin, it traditionally was a way to use up stale bread. I love traditional niçoise salads, and this recipe has some of the same elements (olives and tomatoes), but is more of a modern mash-up of the two styles.

1 large clove GARLIC, halved

3 (1-inch/2.5cm thick) slices day-old crusty WHOLE-WHEAT BREAD

3 tablespoons extra-virgin OLIVE OIL

1 pound (450g) ASPARAGUS, trimmed

½ teaspoon SALT

½ teaspoon freshly ground BLACK PEPPER

2 tablespoons aged BALSAMIC VINEGAR

1 cup (150g) CHERRY TOMATOES, halved

1 cup (240g) low-sodium canned GARBANZO BEANS, rinsed and drained

6 large fresh BASIL leaves, cut into chiffonade

⅓ cup (58g) pitted NIÇOISE or KALAMATA OLIVES

¼ cup (1 ounce/28g) shaved RICOTTA SALATA

1. Preheat a grill or a grill pan to medium.

2. Rub the cut sides of the garlic over both sides of the bread. Use a brush to distribute 1 tablespoon of the oil onto both sides of the bread. Oil the grill or pan and grill the bread on both sides, about 1 minute per side. Transfer to a plate.

3. Sprinkle the asparagus with ¼ teaspoon of the salt and ¼ teaspoon of the pepper. Grill the asparagus for 8 to 10 minutes, until tender. Transfer to a plate.

4. In a large bowl, whisk together the remaining ¼ teaspoon salt and pepper, the remaining 2 tablespoons oil, and the vinegar. Set aside.

5. Cut the grilled bread into 1-inch (2.5cm) cubes and the asparagus into 2-inch (5cm) pieces. Add them to the bowl with the dressing, along with the tomatoes, beans, basil, olives, and ricotta salata. Toss to evenly coat in the vinaigrette and divide among 4 salad bowls.

CALORIES 343

FAT 16.7g
sat 3.2g
mono 10g
poly 1.3g

PROTEIN 13g

CARBOHYDRATES 40g

FIBER 8g

CHOLESTEROL 8mg

IRON 0.5mg

SODIUM 737mg

POTASSIUM 466mg

CALCIUM 151mg

Roasted Fingerling Potato and Smoked Trout Salad

SERVES 4 AS A MAIN COURSE OR 6 AS AN APPETIZER

I'm constantly trying to fit in more servings of fish, so I always keep some canned tuna, salmon, and trout on hand. Like smoked salmon, smoked trout is incredibly flavorful, so a little goes a long way, making it the perfect thing to pair with potatoes. Serve this salad at room temperature with a Sauvignon Blanc and a whole-wheat baguette.

1 pound (450g) FINGERLING POTATOES, such as Ruby Crescents or Russian Bananas, halved

2 tablespoons extra-virgin OLIVE OIL

¼ teaspoon SALT

1 tablespoon whole-grain DIJON MUSTARD

1 tablespoon fresh LEMON JUICE

2 tablespoons WHITE BALSAMIC VINEGAR

1 (3.2-ounce/90g) tin smoked RAINBOW TROUT, skin removed, flaked

2 tablespoons chopped fresh DILL

2 tablespoons chopped fresh flat-leaf PARSLEY leaves

6 cups (400g) BABY SPINACH

1. Preheat the oven to 400ºF (205ºC).

2. In a roasting pan, toss the potatoes with 1 tablespoon of the oil and ⅛ teaspoon of the salt and roast for 40 minutes, until tender.

3. While the potatoes are roasting, whisk together the remaining 1 tablespoon oil and ⅛ teaspoon salt with the mustard and lemon juice in a large bowl. Set aside.

4. When the potatoes are done, immediately transfer them to a large bowl and toss them with the vinegar. Allow the vinegar to be absorbed for 10 minutes. Add the potatoes and any remaining vinegar to the bowl with the mustard mixture; toss gently. Add the trout and herbs and gently toss again.

5. To serve as a dinner salad, divide the greens among 4 bowls and top each with one-quarter of the potato-trout mixture. To serve as a first course, divide the salad among 6 plates.

(as a main course)

CALORIES 206

FAT 8.6g
sat 1.4g
mono 5.7g
poly 1g

PROTEIN 10g

CARBOHYDRATES 24g

FIBER 4g

CHOLESTEROL 32mg

IRON 2mg

SODIUM 290mg

POTASSIUM 664mg

CALCIUM 21mg

Spinach

RECIPES: **Grilled Halloumi and Lemon Salad,** page 88 **Roasted Fingerling Potato and Smoked Trout Salad,** opposite

The basics: It was the Spanish who first brought spinach, a plant native to the Middle East, to the United States.

Seasonality: Spinach is available year-round.

Good stuff: One cup (180g) of raw spinach has a super-slim 7 calories. It's rich in iron—1 cup (30g) of cooked leaves has more than 6mg. Make it easier for your body to absorb this type of plant-based iron by eating it with a vitamin C–rich food, such as citrus fruit or tomatoes.

Pick it: Choose spinach with crisp, dark green leaves and no sign of wetness or damage. You can also purchase the leaves prewashed in bags and plastic boxes.

Store it: Keep spinach in a plastic bag, or in the plastic box it came in, in the refrigerator for up to three days.

Use it: If it isn't prewashed, spinach needs to be washed thoroughly before using. Remove any large stems. Spinach is delicious raw in salads, sandwiches, and wraps. It's excellent sautéed with garlic and then combined with pine nuts and raisins or dried cranberries. Spinach also makes a nice addition to omelets and baked dishes, such as stuffed shells and lasagna.

Herbs

RECIPES: **Watermelon-Cucumber Cooler (aka Hangover Helper)**, page 24 **Salad in a Jar**, page 33 **Grilled Halloumi and Lemon Salad**, page 88 **Golden Beets with Parsley Pesto and Fregola**, page 91 **Curried Chicken Salad with Cashews and Grapes**, page 92 **Minted Peas with Sautéed Shrimp**, page 115 **Roasted Fingerling Potato and Smoked Trout Salad**, page 122 **Italian Barley Salad with Herb Oil**, opposite **Corn and Basil Crab Toasts**, page 129 **Roasted Vegetables with Penne**, page 133 **Green Greek Goddess Dip**, page 140 **Glazed Red Cipollinis**, page 165 **Freekeh Tabbouleh**, page 195

The basics: Herbs are the leaves of various annual and perennial plants that do not have woody stems.

Seasonality: Most herbs can be found year-round.

Good stuff: With their wonderful fragrance, flavor, and color, herbs are a welcome addition to most dishes. They are a great way to boost the flavor of a recipe without adding sodium or extra calories. They also offer a wealth of antioxidants and are easy to grow—even on a windowsill.

Pick it: Look for herbs with a bright, fresh appearance and no sign of wilting or discoloration.

Store it: Wrap fresh herbs lightly in a damp paper towel and store them in a zip-top plastic bag for up to five days. If you will be using them within two to three days, you can trim the ends and place them in a small vase or glass with water.

Use it: Gently rinse herbs before using and blot dry with a clean kitchen towel or paper towels. Chop them to release their oils and therefore their flavor. Most herbs should be added toward the end of the cooking process, but rosemary is hardy enough to be added at the beginning. Though fresh herbs are generally better, you can substitute 1 teaspoon of dried herbs for 1 tablespoon of fresh herbs.

Italian Barley Salad with Herb Oil

SERVES 8

Barley is one of those soul-satisfying grains that doesn't get enough love or attention. True, it does take a while to cook this whole grain, but the chewy, nutty result is so worth it. And if you're looking for a well-balanced vegetarian dish, simply leave the prosciutto out. Want more barley options? Turn to page 185. The herb oil can be made a day in advance.

1 cup (184g) uncooked hulled BARLEY

1 cup (48g) fresh BASIL leaves

½ cup (9g) fresh flat-leaf PARSLEY leaves

1 (9-ounce/250g) package frozen ARTICHOKE HEARTS (2 cups)

¾ cup (175ml) extra-virgin OLIVE OIL

½ teaspoon SALT

1 (15-ounce/425g) can KIDNEY BEANS, rinsed and drained

½ cup (90g) marinated OLIVES, pitted and halved

1 cup (150g) CHERRY TOMATOES, halved

¼ cup (25g) toasted PINE NUTS

⅓ cup (47g) roasted RED PEPPERS, chopped

1 ounce (28g) PROSCIUTTO, sliced (optional)

1. Combine the barley and 2½ cups (600ml) of water in a 2-quart (2L) saucepan and bring to a boil. Reduce the heat and simmer until the barley is tender, about 30 minutes. Remove from the heat and drain any excess water. Transfer to a large bowl and set aside to cool.

2. Meanwhile, bring a small pot of water to a boil and add the basil and parsley. When just wilted (about 10 seconds), remove with a slotted spoon, transfer to a colander, and rinse under cold water. Blot the herbs with paper towels and set aside. To the still-boiling water, add the artichoke hearts and cook for 5 minutes; drain and set aside.

3. In a blender, combine the blanched herbs, oil, and salt and blend until smooth. Pour 2 tablespoons of the herb oil over the barley and stir. Pour another 2 tablespoons of the herb oil over the artichoke hearts.

4. To the barley, add the artichoke hearts, beans, olives, tomatoes, pine nuts, roasted red peppers, and prosciutto, if using. Before serving, drizzle the salad with another 2 tablespoons of the herb oil. Store any leftover herb oil in an airtight container in the refrigerator for up to a week. Bring to room temperature before drizzling over salad, cooked potatoes, or chicken.

CALORIES 380

FAT 25.5g
sat 4g
mono 18g
poly 2.7g

PROTEIN 9g

CARBOHYDRATES 30g

FIBER 9g

CHOLESTEROL 4mg

IRON 2mg

SODIUM 589mg

POTASSIUM 390mg

CALCIUM 63mg

Late Summer Succotash

SERVES 6

Not only is this is an excellent—and filling—vegetarian main dish (mega fiber, iron, potassium, and calcium!), it also makes a great side for grilled steak or chicken. Don't be put off by all of the prep work. If you don't have time to cook the cranberry beans, just pop open a can of cannellini beans instead. And you can always substitute grilled vegetables from your grocery store's prepared foods section to save more time.

¼ cup (60ml) extra-virgin OLIVE OIL

1 teaspoon SALT

¾ teaspoon freshly ground BLACK PEPPER

1 tablespoon fresh LEMON JUICE

2 tablespoons WHITE BALSAMIC VINEGAR

1 pound (450g) fresh CRANBERRY or LIMA BEANS in pods

½ teaspoon KOSHER SALT

1 pound (450g) small POTATOES, such as fingerlings or Red Bliss

2 ANAHEIM PEPPERS, halved and seeded

1 YELLOW BELL PEPPER, quartered and seeded

1 (5- to 6-ounce/150- to 170g) JAPANESE EGGPLANT, halved

1 (12-ounce/340g) bag frozen shelled EDAMAME

¼ cup (30g) CAPERS, rinsed and drained

1. In a large bowl, whisk together 2 tablespoons of the oil, ½ teaspoon of the salt, ¼ teaspoon of the black pepper, the lemon juice, and the vinegar; set aside.

2. Fill a medium saucepan with water and bring to a boil. While the water heats, shell the beans. Add the beans and the kosher salt to the water, return to a boil, and cook for 15 minutes. Using a slotted spoon, transfer the hot beans to the bowl with the vinaigrette. Add the potatoes to the boiling water and cook for 20 minutes, until tender. Drain the potatoes and rinse under cold water until cool. Cut them in half lengthwise and add to the beans.

3. Preheat a grill to high or a grill pan over high heat. Brush the Anaheim and yellow bell peppers and eggplant on both sides with the remaining 2 tablespoons oil. Sprinkle with the remaining ½ teaspoon salt and ½ teaspoon black pepper. Reduce the heat to medium-high, add half of the vegetables, and cook for 5 minutes. Turn the vegetables and cook for 3 minutes more, until tender. Transfer the vegetables to a plate and let cool. Repeat with the remaining vegetables.

4. While the vegetables grill, place the edamame in a microwave-safe bowl and cook for 4 minutes. Drain and toss with the cranberry beans and vinaigrette.

5. When the grilled vegetables are cool enough to handle, cut them into 1-inch (2.5cm) pieces and add them to the bean and potato mixture. Stir in the capers and serve.

CALORIES 492

FAT 14g
sat 2g
mono 6.8g
poly 1.8g

PROTEIN 27g

CARBOHYDRATES 70g

FIBER 24g

CHOLESTEROL 0mg

IRON 6mg

SODIUM 705mg

POTASSIUM 1848mg

CALCIUM 182mg

Corn and Basil Crab Toasts

SERVES 4

If you like the sweet, briny flavor of crab cakes, you will love these toasts. They are incredibly easy to make—even for a last-minute dinner party—and go exceptionally well with rosé wine. The toasts can also be cut into bite-size pieces and served on a platter as a passed appetizer. A *ficelle* is a smaller, thinner style of French bread and works really well for the toasts, but you can also use a baguette.

For the toasts:

1 FICELLE or ½ BAGUETTE

1 AVOCADO, pitted and peeled

2 tablespoons fresh LEMON JUICE

For the spicy mayonnaise:

¼ cup (60g) CANOLA MAYONNAISE

1 teaspoon finely grated LEMON ZEST

¼ teaspoon sweet PAPRIKA

¼ teaspoon ground RED PEPPER

For the crab:

½ pound (225g) jumbo lump CRAB MEAT

1 small ear CORN, cooked and kernels removed, or ⅓ cup (62g) thawed frozen corn kernels

¼ cup (50g) minced ORANGE or RED BELL PEPPER

⅛ teaspoon SALT

⅛ teaspoon freshly ground BLACK PEPPER

1 tablespoon fresh BASIL leaves, torn

1 teaspoon LEMON ZEST

1. Prepare the toasts: Using a serrated bread knife, slice the *ficelle* in half lengthwise and then cut each half crosswise into 4 equal pieces. Lightly toast the bread in a toaster oven. Mash the avocado with the lemon juice and spread it on the toasted bread.

2. Make the spicy mayonnaise: In a small bowl, whisk together all the ingredients and set aside.

3. Make the crab mixture: In a medium bowl, gently combine the ingredients for the crab.

4. Stir the spicy mayonnaise into the crab mixture. Spoon the crab topping onto all 8 toasts and serve 2 per person.

CALORIES 410

FAT 19g
sat 1.6g
mono 12g
poly 4.5g

PROTEIN 21g

CARBOHYDRATES 42g

FIBER 6g

CHOLESTEROL 45mg

IRON 2.6mg

SODIUM 748mg

POTASSIUM 314mg

CALCIUM 51mg

Orecchiette with Snap Peas and Tuna

SERVES 6

We eat a lot of whole-wheat pasta at my house. I mean a *lot*. To break up the tan monotony of so much of it, I make a point of adding something colorful to every pasta meal. I love *orecchiette* because they're so darn cute (the name in Italian means "little ears") and also because they tend to grab and hold sauce very nicely.

1 pound (450g) WHOLE-WHEAT ORECCHIETTE

½ pound (225g) SUGAR SNAP PEAS, trimmed and halved diagonally

½ cup (50g) WALNUTS

½ cup (60g) CAPERS, rinsed and drained

⅛ teaspoon SALT

2 teaspoons finely grated LEMON ZEST

1 teaspoon fresh LEMON JUICE

2 tablespoons extra-virgin OLIVE OIL, plus more for serving

2 tablespoons grated PARMESAN

1 (4.4-ounce/125g) can TUNA, drained

¼ cup (10g) chopped fresh flat-leaf PARSLEY leaves

1. Bring a large pot of salted water to a boil. Cook the orecchiette according to the package directions. Steam the snap peas for 2 minutes, just until the color brightens. Transfer the peas to a bowl. (If you have a steamer basket that's larger than the diameter of your pasta-cooking pot, you can set it directly on top and utilize the steam rising off the boiling water below—saving energy and pan-washing time. This also works well with a 3-in-1 style pot.)

2. While the pasta is cooking, combine the walnuts, capers, salt, lemon zest, lemon juice, oil, and cheese in a food processor or blender and process until smooth.

3. Drain the pasta, reserving ¼ cup (60ml) of the cooking water. In a large bowl, toss the hot pasta with the walnut mixture, adding a little of the cooking water if more moisture is needed. Break up the tuna and add it to the bowl; toss again. Finally, add the snap peas and parsley and toss one last time before serving. If you like, drizzle a bit more oil over the pasta before you plate it. Serve warm or at room temperature.

CALORIES 444

FAT 14g
sat 2g
mono 4.9g
poly 5.7g

PROTEIN 19g

CARBOHYDRATES 61g

FIBER 4.5g

CHOLESTEROL 8mg

IRON 4mg

SODIUM 520mg

POTASSIUM 371mg

CALCIUM 84mg

Sugar Snap Peas

RECIPES: **Orecchiette with Snap Peas and Tuna,** opposite **Roasted Vegetables with Penne,** page 133

The basics: This sweet vegetable is a cross between the English pea and snow peas. The pod and the peas inside can be eaten, which makes it especially good for snacking. Some sugar snaps have strings that need to be removed before using them, but some varieties are stringless.

Seasonality: Sugar snaps are available year-round.

Good stuff: Crunchy and sweet, sugar snaps are a favorite with kids. A 1-cup (100g) serving has 31 calories, nearly 3g of fiber, and supplies folate and vitamin B6.

Pick it: Look for firm, juicy-looking pods with a bright green color and no signs of dryness or yellowing.

Store it: Keep sugar snaps in a plastic bag in the refrigerator for up to three days.

Use it: Sugar snaps can be enjoyed raw or cooked briefly. They're delicious in stir-fries and can be microwaved and steamed as well. They're also nice just blanched and tossed with cooked pasta or grains. Try serving them on a crudité platter—they make great dippers.

Zucchini

RECIPES: **Classic Marinara with Zucchini,** page 34 **Roasted Vegetables with Penne,** opposite

The basics: Zucchini is a summer squash with skin that ranges from dark to light green, and it may have yellow markings or stripes. The skin is thin, tender, and edible—so are the seeds—especially when the squash is on the smaller side. Zucchini blossoms are also edible and are delicious stuffed.

Seasonality: Zucchini is grown year-round, but the peak season is summer.

Good stuff: A 1-cup (180g) serving of cooked zucchini is a slim 27 calories. Zucchini is rich in the antioxidants lutein and zeaxanthin, which are important for eye health and may help prevent macular degeneration. The vegetable also contains pectin, which aids in stabilizing blood sugar.

Pick it: Choose firm zucchini with smooth skin. It should be free of marks or cuts.

Store it: It's preferable to keep zucchini in a cool spot in your kitchen in a perforated plastic bag for a few days. You can also store it in the refrigerator for up to four days.

Use it: Zucchini is quick cooking and doesn't take much to be tasty. A simple sauté with garlic and onions is wonderful, and you can also grill, roast, steam, or fry it. Zucchini adds moisture and flavor to muffins and quick breads and you can also shave it with a vegetable peeler for a raw salad tossed with lemon and olive oil. Oven-baked zucchini chips are a tasty spin on the traditional potato chip.

Roasted Vegetables with Penne

SERVES 6

Since life with kids is never uninterrupted, I'm a big fan of recipes that can be made in stages. This one is no exception. I usually roast the vegetables in the morning, and then cook the pasta just before serving. However you make it, it's an easy weeknight dinner, and the leftovers make an excellent bring-to-work pasta salad. If you don't add the Manchego, it's a completely vegan dish.

2 small ZUCCHINI, sliced into ⅛-inch (3mm) rounds (1¼ cups)

10 BABY CARROTS, halved lengthwise

1 RED ONION, cut into 1-inch (2.5cm) chunks

2 tablespoons extra-virgin OLIVE OIL

¼ teaspoon SALT

¼ teaspoon freshly ground BLACK PEPPER

2 cups (120g) SUGAR SNAP PEAS, trimmed

1 pound (450g) WHOLE-WHEAT PENNE or RIGATONI

½ cup shaved MANCHEGO CHEESE (about 1½ ounces/42g), shaved with a vegetable peeler

2 tablespoons fresh BASIL leaves, torn

1. Preheat the oven to 375ºF (190ºC). Bring a large pot of salted water to a boil.

2. Place the zucchini, carrots, and onion in a large roasting pan, drizzle with 1 tablespoon of the oil, sprinkle with ⅛ teaspoon each of the salt and pepper, and roast for 20 minutes more. Add the peas and roast 20 minutes more, until the carrots are tender. About 10 minutes after you've added the peas, add the pasta to the boiling water and cook according to the package directions. Drain.

3. Place the hot pasta in a large serving bowl and toss with the remaining 1 tablespoon oil and remaining ⅛ teaspoon each of salt and pepper. Add the roasted vegetables, cheese, and basil, and toss again.

CALORIES 450

FAT 15.5g
sat 6.7g
mono 3.6g
poly 0.5g

PROTEIN 16g

CARBOHYDRATES 61g

FIBER 8g

CHOLESTEROL 26mg

IRON 3mg

SODIUM 211mg

POTASSIUM 416mg

CALCIUM 47mg

Spicy Brown Rice Bowl with Chard

SERVES 5

I've always loved the Korean dish *bibimbap*. There was a Korean restaurant in my college town, Ithaca, New York, and I'd treat myself to a satisfying bowl of *bibimbap* once exams were over. Traditionally, the dish combines brown rice with sautéed spinach, a small amount of beef, and an assortment of seasoned vegetables. All of the items are presented in a hot bowl, and diners then top the ingredients with the accompanying (and addictive) spicy red sauce. It's often topped with a fried egg. I've simplified the dish and made it even healthier—swapping out cooked chicken for the beef, and Swiss chard for the spinach.

1 cup (200g) BROWN RICE

For the sauce:

2 teaspoons toasted SESAME OIL

2 teaspoons SRIRACHA HOT CHILI SAUCE

1 teaspoon low-sodium SOY SAUCE

1 tablespoon plus 1 teaspoon fresh LEMON JUICE

1 teaspoon OLIVE OIL

1 bunch (1 pound/353g) rainbow SWISS CHARD leaves and stems, chopped

⅛ teaspoon SALT

2 SCALLIONS, sliced, green parts only

2 medium RADISHES, sliced

1¼ cups (155g) cooked CHICKEN, chopped

COOKING SPRAY, for the pan

5 large EGGS

1. Cook the rice according to the package directions.

2. Make the sauce: In a small bowl, whisk together the sesame oil, Sriracha, soy sauce, and lemon juice. Set aside.

3. Heat the olive oil in a large sauté pan over medium–high heat and add the chard. Sprinkle with the salt and cook for 8 to 10 minutes, until completely wilted. Remove from the heat and set aside.

4. To serve, in each of 5 bowls, place ½ cup (125g) of the cooked rice, ½ cup (90g) of the chard, 1 teaspoon of the scallion, about 4 slices of the radish, and ¼ cup (30g) of the chicken.

5. Spray a large sauté pan with cooking spray and fry the eggs in batches over high heat to the desired degree of doneness (add more spray to the pan as needed). I prefer cooking them for about 2 minutes each, until the whites are firm and the yolks are still slightly runny. Transfer 1 egg to each bowl. Drizzle each serving with 1 teaspoon of the sauce and serve while the egg is hot.

CALORIES 372

FAT 12g
sat 3.2g
mono 5g
poly 3g

PROTEIN 33g

CARBOHYDRATES 30g

FIBER 2g

CHOLESTEROL 251mg

IRON 2.6mg

SODIUM 300mg

POTASSIUM 419mg

CALCIUM 59mg

Edamame

RECIPE: **Late Summer Succotash,** page 126

The basics: Edamame are young, fresh soybeans still in the pod. They are often served boiled in Japanese restaurants as a side dish with sea salt on top.

Seasonality: Fresh edamame can be found in early fall. You can find them frozen year-round.

Good stuff: High in fiber, protein, and folate, edamame are super-nutritious. They provide all the essential amino acids, so they're a great addition to vegetarian diets. Soy contains isoflavones, which may help reduce the severity of menopausal symptoms and decrease the risk of osteoporosis. They also help keep your heart healthy by lowering cholesterol levels and may help reduce the risk of prostate cancer.

Pick it: It's unusual to find fresh edamame at the grocery store, but you may find it at a farmer's market. It's easy to find both edamame in the pod and shelled edamame in bags in the frozen section of the grocery store. Either form should be bright green in color.

Store it: If you do find fresh edamame, store it in the refrigerator for three to four days. Frozen edamame will last for several months.

Use it: Whole edamame can be boiled with 2 tablespoons of salt for 3 to 4 minutes and then drained. You can add more sea salt to taste on top of the beans. If using fresh edamame, trim the stem end first. Once cooked, you can use shelled edamame in salads, soups, and spreads. While they can be cooked in the pod, the pod of the soybean is not edible.

Cucumbers

The basics: As members of the gourd family, cucumbers hail from either India or Thailand, and have been cultivated for thousands of years. Cukes grow on a creeping vine and are botanically categorized as fruit. American cucumbers are rounder and have tougher (though still edible) seeds than Asian or European varieties. The skin of American cucumbers is often waxed and should be peeled before eating. The English, or hothouse, variety is longer and has small, soft seeds that needn't be removed. (This is why, somewhat confusingly, the variety is referred to as "seedless.") You'll find English cucumbers wrapped in plastic because their thin, unwaxed skins are easily bruised; the unwaxed skin can be eaten. Kirby cucumbers are only 3 to 6 inches (7.5 to 15cm) long, have somewhat bumpy skin, and are also known as pickling cucumbers. You may also find other cucumber varieties at your local farmer's market, such as Armenian and Persian, as well as lemon, which indeed look like the citrus fruit.

Seasonality: American and English, or "hothouse," cucumbers are grown year-round. Their season peaks from May through August. You'll only find Kirby cukes and the other varieties during the summer.

Good stuff: There's a reason why cucumbers are often associated with spas—at 96 percent water, they're incredibly hydrating. Cucumbers contain caffeic acid, an antioxidant that helps fight swelling. The green gourds are also rich in the mineral silica, which is touted for keeping skin healthy. And 1 cup (104g) of sliced cucumber with the peel on has a skimpy 16 calories! So it's great for snacking and adding to sandwiches and salads for added no-guilt crunch.

Pick it: Look for cucumbers (American and English) with smooth, firm, uniformly colored skin. Kirby cucumbers can have bumpy skin and vary in color from light yellow to green. No matter what the variety, there should be no soft spots or indentations.

Store it: Keep cucumbers in a plastic bag in the refrigerator for up to ten days. Rinse well just before using. Keep away from the rear of the refrigerator, which has a tendency to freeze items with a high water content.

Use it: If using a waxed cucumber, make sure to peel it first. Other cukes can be eaten skin and all. If your cucumber has large, firm seeds, scoop them out before using it in a recipe. Due to their high water content, cucumbers can't be cooked and should only be enjoyed raw. They are a crunchy addition to salads and are delicious in cold soups and dips.

Mustard-Crusted Pork Tenderloin with Napa Cabbage and Apple Slaw

SERVES 6

Pork tenderloin is not only really easy to make, it's also incredibly lean and healthy. And the sweet, crunchy slaw makes a delicious foil for the mustardy pork.

¼ cup WHOLE-GRAIN DIJON MUSTARD

¼ cup DIJON MUSTARD

1 tablespoon low-sodium SOY SAUCE

1 tablespoon pure MAPLE SYRUP

1½ pounds (700g) PORK TENDERLOIN (about 2 tenderloins)

2 tablespoons OLIVE OIL

For the slaw:

1 head NAPA CABBAGE, chopped (5 cups/350g)

2 FUJI or PINK LADY APPLES, cored and sliced into thin wedges (2½ cups/250g)

½ cup (9g) fresh flat-leaf PARSLEY leaves, chopped

Juice of 1 LEMON

2 tablespoons HONEY

2 tablespoons APPLE CIDER VINEGAR

¼ teaspoon SALT

¼ teaspoon freshly ground BLACK PEPPER

½ cup (125ml) APPLE CIDER for deglazing pan

1. In a small bowl, whisk together the mustards, soy sauce, and maple syrup. Place the pork in a large zip-top bag or shallow dish and thoroughly coat it with the mustard mixture. Cover and refrigerate for 1 to 3 hours.

2. While the pork is marinating, make the slaw: Place the cabbage, apple, and parsley in a large serving bowl and toss to combine. In a small bowl, whisk together the lemon juice, honey, vinegar, salt, and pepper and drizzle over the cabbage mixture. Cover and refrigerate until ready to serve.

3. Preheat the oven to 400ºF (205ºC). Heat the oil in a large ovenproof sauté pan over medium-high heat. Add the pork and cook for 4 minutes on each side, until browned. Transfer the sauté pan to the oven and roast for 15 minutes, until a meat thermometer inserted into the pork registers 165ºF (74ºC).

4. Transfer the pork to a cutting board and let it rest for 5 to 10 minutes before slicing, so the juices don't escape.

5. Meanwhile, add the cider to the sauté pan and heat over high, scraping up any browned bits in the pan, until the liquid reduces by half, about 5 minutes.

6. On each plate, place 3 slices of the pork and 1½ cups (125g) of the slaw. Drizzle about 1 tablespoon of the pan sauce over each serving of pork and serve.

CALORIES 257

FAT 7.3g
sat 1.5g
mono 4.3g
poly 1.1g

PROTEIN 25g

CARBOHYDRATES 22g

FIBER 2g

CHOLESTEROL 73mg

IRON 1.5mg

SODIUM 637mg

POTASSIUM 549mg

CALCIUM 53mg

Lamb Sliders with Tzatziki

MAKES 12 SLIDERS

Lamb tends to be polarizing—you either love it or hate it. We love it. I find that because it's so naturally flavorful, you really don't need to do much to it. I don't have a full-size grill right now, and these sliders make me miss it more than I can say, but a grill pan still produces really excellent results.

For the tzatziki:

1 large CUCUMBER, peeled, seeded and finely diced (1½ cups/225g)

¾ cup (175g) fat-free PLAIN GREEK YOGURT

1 tablespoon fresh LEMON JUICE

⅛ teaspoon SALT

⅛ teaspoon ground WHITE PEPPER

1 large clove GARLIC, minced

2 tablespoons chopped fresh flat-leaf PARSLEY leaves

For the lamb sliders:

COOKING SPRAY, for the pan

1 pound (450g) ground LAMB

⅛ teaspoon ground CUMIN

⅛ teaspoon dried OREGANO

¼ teaspoon ground WHITE PEPPER

¼ teaspoon SALT

1 SHALLOT, minced

12 small BUNS, about 2 inches (5cm) in diameter, split and toasted

1. Combine all the tzatziki ingredients in a medium bowl. Cover and refrigerate until ready to serve.

2. Make the lamb sliders: Preheat a grill or grill pan to medium-high and coat with cooking spray. Combine the lamb, cumin, oregano, white pepper, salt, and shallot in a large bowl. With clean hands, form the meat into 2-inch (5cm) patties and place on a large plate or platter. Press your thumb into the center of each patty to make an indentation.

3. Set a clean plate or platter nearby for the cooked sliders. Place the sliders on the hot grill and cook for 2 minutes per side (the meat should reach an internal temperature of 160°F/71°C). Transfer the cooked sliders to the clean plate and continue cooking the remaining sliders.

4. Place the cooked sliders on the buns and serve each with a heaping tablespoon of the tzatziki.

(per slider)

CALORIES 250

FAT 12g
sat 3.9g
mono 3.6g
poly 0.7g

PROTEIN 13g

CARBOHYDRATES 22g

FIBER 2g

CHOLESTEROL 28mg

IRON 1mg

SODIUM 277mg

POTASSIUM 130mg

CALCIUM 21mg

Green Greek Goddess Dip

SERVES 6

This is my variation on the famous Green Goddess dressing that is said to have originated at San Francisco's Palace Hotel in 1923. The traditional dressing includes sour cream, anchovies, and just a few herbs. I go over the top on the greens, but just use whatever you have on hand. I like to serve this dip with fresh crudités and whole-grain tortilla or pita chips.

1 cup (230g) fat-free PLAIN GREEK YOGURT

¼ cup (60g) CANOLA MAYONNAISE

Finely grated zest and juice of 1 LEMON

2 tablespoons fresh TARRAGON leaves

2 tablespoons fresh CHIVES

2 tablespoons fresh BASIL leaves

2 tablespoons fresh THYME leaves

2 tablespoons fresh flat-leaf PARSLEY leaves

2 tablespoons fresh CILANTRO leaves

¼ teaspoon SALT

1. Combine all the ingredients in a blender or food processor. Blend until the mixture is creamy, but flecks of herbs are still visible.

2. Cover and refrigerate until ready to serve. The dip keeps in the refrigerator for up to 3 days.

CALORIES 95

FAT 7.5g
sat 0.4g
mono 4.7g
poly 2.4g

PROTEIN 4g

CARBOHYDRATES 3g

FIBER 0g

CHOLESTEROL 3mg

IRON 0.8mg

SODIUM 173mg

POTASSIUM 75mg

CALCIUM 53mg

Arugula

RECIPE: **Scallops with Bacon over Linguini and Arugula,** page 145

The basics: Arugula is an annual plant, also known in Australia, New Zealand, England, and South Africa as rocket. It is related to radishes, watercress, and mustard.

Seasonality: Arugula grows nearly year-round in the United States.

Good stuff: The intense, peppery flavor of arugula leaves is quite polarizing. It's rich in iron, folate, and vitamin A. One cup (20g) of the leaves has just 5 calories.

Pick it: Arugula leaves should be a deep green and without any spots or yellowing.

Store it: Arugula should be used soon after it's purchased, within two to three days. Keep it in the refrigerator in a plastic bag with room for air to circulate.

Use it: Wash arugula leaves well just before using. It's delicious raw in salads, and can also be lightly sautéed. You can also use arugula in place of basil for a twist on pesto.

Lime

The basics: Limes made a name for themselves by helping British sailors fend off scurvy while out at sea. They are grown in tropical and subtropical areas including Mexico, California, Florida, and the Caribbean. There are two main varieties: Persian and Key. Persian limes are the typical type you'll see at the grocery store. Key limes are grown in Florida and are smaller and more yellow; the juice is prized for making pie. The leaves of the kaffir lime are used in Southeast Asian cuisine.

Seasonality: Though limes can be found year-round, they peak from May through August.

Good stuff: The juice of one lime has 15 percent of the vitamin C you need daily.

Pick it: Look for limes that are firm and heavy for their size with bright green skin that shows no signs of wrinkling. It's fine if they have brown patches from the sun—it won't affect their flavor or juiciness.

Store it: Keep whole limes in a plastic bag in the refrigerator for up to ten days. Once sliced into, wrap them tightly in plastic and store for a couple of days.

Use it: Lime zest is incredibly aromatic and is a wonderful way to add interest to a dish without adding salt or oil. The juice is delicious and refreshing in dressings, desserts, drinks, and marinades, and can even "cook" seafood to make ceviche. I love adding fresh lime juice to sparkling water and having my own little "spa moment."

Cilantro-Lime Butter

MAKES ½ CUP (113G)

A compound butter is just a fancy term for butter blended with other things. Compound butters are really easy to make and are a great way to impress company. This one is amazing melted over hot corn on the cob, and it would be equally welcome on warm cornbread or rolls.

½ cup (1 stick/113g) UNSALTED BUTTER, cut into pieces

½ cup (20g) fresh CILANTRO leaves

2 teaspoons finely grated LIME ZEST

1. In a food processor, combine all of the ingredients. Pulse until the mixture is blended, but you can still see pieces of the cilantro.

2. Transfer the compound butter to a piece of plastic wrap and roll it up, twisting the ends to form a log. Refrigerate until firm. Simply remove from the plastic and slice to use. Store in the refrigerator for up to 1 week.

(per tablespoon)

CALORIES 51

FAT 5.8g
sat 3.7g
mono 1.5g
poly 0.2g

PROTEIN 0g

CARBOHYDRATES 0g

FIBER 0g

CHOLESTEROL 0mg

IRON 0.5mg

SODIUM 0.8mg

POTASSIUM 2mg

CALCIUM 2mg

Scallops with Bacon over Linguini and Arugula

SERVES 4

The key to getting a nice golden scallop is twofold: 1. The surface of the scallops must be really dry. 2. The oil in your pan needs to be hot. If you've got those two things going on, you'll have success! And since scallops are so low in fat and calories, you have plenty of room for a bit of bacon.

8 ounces (225g) LINGUINI

12 SEA SCALLOPS (about 1 pound/450g)

¼ teaspoon SALT

¼ teaspoon freshly ground BLACK PEPPER

1 slice center-cut MAPLE BACON, diced (see Note)

1 large clove GARLIC, minced

2 tablespoons fresh LEMON JUICE

4 cups (110g) BABY ARUGULA

1. Bring a large pot of salted water to a boil and cook the linguini according to the package directions. Pat the scallops dry with paper towels, then season them on both sides with the salt and pepper.

2. While the pasta cooks, cook the bacon in a large sauté pan over medium-high heat for 2 to 3 minutes, until the fat renders. Push the bacon to the side with a spatula and add the garlic. Cook the garlic for 1 minute and then add the scallops. Cook the scallops for 2 to 3 minutes on each side, until golden. Transfer the scallops, garlic, and bacon to a platter and keep warm. Wipe the pan clean with a paper towel and set aside for use later.

3. Drain the pasta, reserving ¼ cup (60ml) of the cooking liquid. Add the reserved pasta water to the pan in which you cooked the scallops, along with the lemon juice. Cook over high heat for 2 minutes, until reduced by half.

4. Into each of 4 shallow bowls, place 1 cup of the arugula and 1 cup of the hot linguini. Top each serving with 3 scallops and some of the bacon, then drizzle with a bit of the pan sauce. Serve hot.

NOTE: Center-cut bacon is the bacon that is cut from part of the pig that is closer to the bone and has 20 percent less saturated fat than regular bacon. I like using Niman Ranch Uncured Maple Bacon, which is center-cut bacon that does not have nitrates or nitrites added.

CALORIES 299

FAT 2g
sat 0.41g
mono 0.06g
poly 0.18g

PROTEIN 21g

CARBOHYDRATES 46g

FIBER 1.2g

CHOLESTEROL 29mg

IRON 1.3mg

SODIUM 626mg

POTASSIUM 277mg

CALCIUM 23mg

Matcha Panna Cotta

SERVES 6

Matcha, made by grinding up dried green tea leaves to a powdery consistency, has a distinct earthy, sweet flavor that carries through in this creamy panna cotta. And since you consume the leaf directly in this dessert, instead of brewing it, the antioxidant levels are even higher.

1 cup (250ml) WHOLE MILK

1 (¼-ounce/7g) envelope plain GELATIN

1 cup (250ml) WHIPPING CREAM

2 tablespoons MATCHA (unsweetened green tea powder; see Note)

½ cup (100g) plus 1 tablespoon SUGAR

1 VANILLA BEAN, split

1½ cups (370g) WHOLE MILK VANILLA YOGURT

1 cup (125g) fresh RASPBERRIES

2 tablespoons CHIA SEEDS (optional)

1. Pour ½ cup (125ml) of the milk into a small bowl and sprinkle the gelatin on top. Set aside for 15 minutes to soften.

2. In a large saucepan, combine the remaining ½ cup milk, the whipping cream, matcha, and ½ cup of the sugar. Scrape the seeds from the vanilla bean into the pan and add the empty pod. Bring the mixture to a simmer over medium heat, whisking until the sugar dissolves. Remove from the heat and let steep for 10 minutes.

3. Strain the matcha mixture through a fine-mesh sieve into a medium bowl, then stir in the reserved gelatin mixture. When the matcha mixture has cooled, add the yogurt and stir to combine; set aside.

4. Using a fork, mash the berries with the remaining 1 tablespoon sugar in a small bowl. Mix in the chia seeds, if using.

5. Into the bottom of 6 small juice glasses or dessert wine glasses, spoon 1 tablespoon of the mashed berries. Slowly pour ½ cup (125ml) of the matcha mixture into each glass. Refrigerate for 3 to 6 hours, until set.

NOTE: Matcha can be quite expensive, so it makes sense to invest in one that you like and will use often. The Republic of Tea makes one called U Matcha in various flavors. Get the "natural" one, which has the most pure, sweet green tea leaf flavor. In addition to using it in this yummy panna cotta, I like having a cup of matcha to perk up after lunch.

CALORIES 317

FAT 19g
sat 11g
mono 5g
poly 2g

PROTEIN 10g

CARBOHYDRATES 33g

FIBER 3g

CHOLESTEROL 67mg

IRON 0.5mg

SODIUM 64mg

POTASSIUM 224mg

CALCIUM 174mg

Blues, Indigos & Violets

The deep, jewel-toned colors in this family are reason alone to enjoy them. On top of that, they deliver high amounts of anthocyanins, a type of antioxidant that fights inflammation and may help reduce the risk of heart disease and cancer. And certain members of this gorgeous crew may also help keep your memory sharp and boost your brainpower. I say bring on the blues!

Double Blue Scones

MAKES 8 SCONES

My first experience making scones was—believe it or not—on an island in the Great Barrier Reef. I was on a scuba excursion that was set up through the university I was attending in New South Wales, Australia. While staying on Lady Musgrave Island, the small boat we were using to take us out into deeper waters drifted away, so we had plenty of time on our hands to cook. I don't recall exactly how we managed to make the scones, but I do remember that they had dates in them and were delicious. This version is equally good, and you don't need to be stranded on an island to enjoy them.

1 cup (155g) old-fashioned ROLLED OATS

1½ cups (180g) ALL-PURPOSE FLOUR

½ cup (100g) SUGAR

2 teaspoons BAKING POWDER

½ teaspoon BAKING SODA

¼ teaspoon SALT

½ cup (1 stick/113g) UNSALTED BUTTER, cut into small pieces

½ cup (63g) fresh or frozen and thawed BLUEBERRIES

⅓ cup (70g) dried BLUEBERRIES

Finely grated zest of 1 large LEMON

1 teaspoon pure VANILLA EXTRACT

¼ cup (60ml) 2% MILK

2 tablespoons DEMERARA SUGAR or other coarse sugar

1. Preheat the oven to 350°F (177°C). Line a baking sheet with parchment paper.

2. Combine the oats, flour, sugar, baking powder, baking soda, and salt in a food processor and blend until combined. Add the butter and pulse until the mixture resembles coarse meal.

3. In a small bowl, combine the fresh or frozen blueberries, dried blueberries, lemon zest, vanilla, and milk. Transfer the flour-butter mixture to a large mixing bowl and gently fold in the blueberry mixture. Using clean hands, form the dough into a disc 1¼ inches (3cm) thick.

4. Place the dough on the lined baking sheet and use a knife to slice it into 8 equal wedges. Sprinkle with the demerara sugar.

5. Bake the scones for 25 minutes, until light golden. You may need to cut in between the scones again for them to separate before serving.

CALORIES 310

FAT 13g
sat 7.5g
mono 3.3g
poly 0.7g

PROTEIN 4g

CARBOHYDRATES 45g

FIBER 3g

CHOLESTEROL 32mg

IRON 3.1mg

SODIUM 294mg

POTASSIUM 55mg

CALCIUM 23mg

Triple Berry Sauce

MAKES 1¾ CUPS (400ML)

Need something to jazz up your buckwheat flapjacks (page 154)? This sauce is so simple to make, but incredibly delicious. It's a great way to add flavor to plain yogurt—even little ones will eat yogurt when it has a sweet berry swirl. You can use either fresh or frozen berries. If you're using fresh berries, wash them well right before starting the recipe.

1 cup (125g) fresh or frozen BLUEBERRIES

1 cup (125g) fresh or frozen RASPBERRIES

1 cup (115g) fresh STRAWBERRIES, hulled and sliced, or frozen strawberries

½ cup (125ml) pure MAPLE SYRUP

1 teaspoon pure VANILLA EXTRACT

1. Put the berries—with water still clinging to them, if using fresh berries—in a medium saucepan over medium-high heat. Pour in the maple syrup, cover, and bring to a simmer. Simmer for 8 to 10 minutes, stirring occasionally. Turn the heat off, stir in the vanilla, and skim off any foam that may have risen.

2. Serve warm over pancakes, waffles, ice cream, or yogurt, or transfer to an airtight container and chill. The sauce will keep for 3 days in the refrigerator.

CALORIES 56

FAT 0.19g
sat 0.01g
mono 0.02g
poly 0.1g

PROTEIN 0.4g

CARBOHYDRATES 14g

FIBER 1.5g

CHOLESTEROL 0mg

IRON 0.2mg

SODIUM 2mg

POTASSIUM 82mg

CALCIUM 20mg

Willa's Buckwheat Flapjacks

MAKES 18 FLAPJACKS

I think my daughter, Willa, picked up the word flapjack from the Little Bear series created by Maurice Sendak. While I don't think there's any distinction between a pancake and a flapjack, I have to agree with Willa that the latter is somehow more enticing.

1 cup (160g) BUCKWHEAT FLOUR

1 cup (120g) ALL-PURPOSE FLOUR

1 teaspoon BAKING SODA

1 teaspoon ground CINNAMON

3 tablespoons LIGHT BROWN SUGAR

¼ teaspoon SALT

1¾ cups (415ml) 2% MILK

¼ cup (60ml) CANOLA OIL

1 large EGG, whisked

COOKING SPRAY, for the pan

TRIPLE BERRY SAUCE (page 153), for serving

1. Combine the flours, baking soda, cinnamon, brown sugar, and salt in a large bowl. In a separate bowl, whisk together the milk, oil, and egg. Make a well in the dry ingredients and stir in half of the wet mixture. Add the remaining wet mixture and combine thoroughly.

2. Spray a large nonstick sauté pan with cooking spray and heat over medium-high heat. Using a ¼-cup (60ml) measure, spoon the batter onto the hot pan. Cook each flapjack for 3 minutes, until bubbles begin to form on the surface, then flip and cook for another 2 minutes.

3. Serve the flapjacks with the Triple Berry Sauce.

(per 3 flapjacks)

CALORIES 322

FAT 13g
sat 2.6g
mono 7g
poly 3g

PROTEIN 10g

CARBOHYDRATES 40g

FIBER 4g

CHOLESTEROL 42mg

IRON 1mg

SODIUM 383mg

POTASSIUM 318mg

CALCIUM 177mg

Three-Berry Oat Bars

MAKES 16 BARS

I like having a homemade snack around the house to quell after-school and after-work munchies. I want it to be healthy, but to still feel like a treat. These bars meet all of my requirements and they're also really easy to make, which is always a plus in my book.

½ cup (62g) WHOLE-WHEAT FLOUR

½ cup (60g) ALL-PURPOSE FLOUR

1 cup (155g) old-fashioned ROLLED OATS

¼ teaspoon BAKING SODA

¼ teaspoon SALT

1 teaspoon ground CINNAMON

½ cup (115g) packed LIGHT BROWN SUGAR

1 cup WHOLE MILK VANILLA YOGURT

¼ cup (½ stick/57g) UNSALTED BUTTER, chilled, cut into small pieces

1 cup (125g) fresh RASPBERRIES

1 cup (125g) fresh BLUEBERRIES

1 cup (120g) fresh BLACKBERRIES

¼ cup (50g) SUGAR

1 tablespoon CORNSTARCH

1 teaspoon finely grated LEMON ZEST

1. Preheat the oven to 350ºF (177ºC).

2. Combine the flours, oats, baking soda, salt, cinnamon, and brown sugar in a large bowl. Stir in the yogurt, then mix in the butter with clean hands. The mixture will be thick and porridgelike.

3. Set aside ¾ cup of the oat mixture. Place the remaining mixture into an 8-inch (20cm) square baking dish and spread it evenly to the edges with a spatula.

4. Combine the berries with the sugar, cornstarch, and lemon zest in a bowl. Pour the berry mixture into the baking dish and sprinkle the reserved oat mixture evenly over the top. Bake for 40 minutes, until the topping is set and the berries are bubbling. Let cool for 20 to 30 minutes before slicing into 16 bars.

CALORIES 125

FAT 3.5g
sat 1.9g
mono 0.9g
poly 0.4g

PROTEIN 2g

CARBOHYDRATES 23g

FIBER 2g

CHOLESTEROL 8mg

IRON 0.6mg

SODIUM 59mg

POTASSIUM 62mg

CALCIUM 15mg

Blueberry Salsa

When blueberries are in season, I can't get enough of them. Not only are they incredibly good for you, their flavor is one I never seem to tire of. This spicy–sweet salsa is of course excellent with tortilla chips, and it also goes well with grilled chicken, fish, or pork.

1 pint (250g) fresh BLUEBERRIES

¼ medium RED ONION, diced

¼ cup (10g) fresh CILANTRO leaves, chopped

Juice of 1 LIME

1 small JALAPEÑO, seeded and minced

¼ teaspoon SALT

Chop 1 cup (125g) of the blueberries. In a medium bowl, gently combine the chopped blueberries and the remaining whole blueberries with the onion, cilantro, lime juice, jalapeño, and salt. The salsa will keep for 1 day in the refrigerator.

CALORIES 20

FAT 0.11g
sat 0.01g
mono 0.02g
poly 0.05g

PROTEIN 0.3g

CARBOHYDRATES 5g

FIBER 0.8g

CHOLESTEROL 0mg

IRON 0.1mg

SODIUM 59mg

POTASSIUM 36mg

CALCIUM 3mg

Blueberries

RECIPES: **Double Blue Scones,** page 150 **Triple Berry Sauce,** page 153 **Three-Berry Oat Bars,** page 155 **Blueberry Salsa,** opposite **Pumpkin Seed-Chia Granola with Mango,** page 178

The basics: This sweet summer favorite grows on bushes and is native to North America. The "lowbush" variety is the wild blueberry, which is smaller in size, often more intensely flavored, and grown mostly in Maine. The "high-bush" variety produces larger, plumper berries and is grown in New Jersey, Oregon, North Carolina, Georgia, and Washington.

Seasonality: Blueberry season lasts from late May though early October in the United States. South American blue-berries can be purchased from November through March.

Good stuff: Blueberries are a darling in the world of health research. Thanks to their polyphenol content (including anthocyanins), they have proven to be quite promising for helping to reverse age-related declines in cognitive and motor function. While both the lowbush and highbush varieties appear to have these benefits, each group touts the benefits of their variety. I say eat them both! You can't really find the wild ones fresh, but they're easy to find dried and frozen and work great in recipes. The anthocyanin content in blueberries may also help women cut their risk of having a heart attack by a third. A study done by the Harvard School of Public Health and the University of East Anglia in the United Kingdom found that women (ages 25 to 42) who ate three or more cups of blueberries and strawberries each week were 32 percent less likely to have a heart attack than women who only ate the berries once a month or less.

Pick it: Choose deeply colored, firm berries that are uniform in size and have no signs of mold or shriveling. Blueberries often have a silvery bloom, which is perfectly natural.

Store it: Keep blueberries in an airtight container in the refrigerator for up to five days.

Use it: Wash blueberries just before using them. They are delicious as a snack, over yogurt and cereal, and in baked goods. You can also use them in savory recipes, such as grain dishes and sauces for pork, duck, and poultry. They can also be used in cold soups, smoothies, and frozen desserts.

Eggplant

RECIPES: **Roasted Eggplant and Sweet Potato Dip,** page 74 **Late Summer Succotash,** page 126 **Press-to Pesto Picnic Sandwich,** page 199

The basics: This is another example of a fruit masquerading as a vegetable. Specifically, eggplant is a berry that's related to the tomato and potato. There are several eggplant varieties, from the large pear-shaped fruit with dark, glossy skin to white eggplants, which demonstrate how the fruit got its name. There are also the slender light purple Japanese eggplants and the smaller Italian eggplants, which look like a petite version of the most common variety.

Seasonality: Eggplant can be found year-round, but the season peaks in the summer, from August to September.

Good stuff: Eggplant is kind of like tequila—lots of people have a bad experience with it and swear it off forever. I've had unsavory brushes with it too, but I've given it a second chance and I hope you will too. When cooked properly, eggplant is melt-in-your-mouth tender, flavorful, and healthy. At only 35 calories per cup (99g), you can easily make a very filling dish with eggplant that doesn't make you burst at the seams. Beyond that, the skin of the eggplant contains nasunin, a plant pigment that has been shown to help protect cell membranes from damage in animal studies.

Pick it: Eggplants should have smooth, glossy skin and should feel heavy for their size. Avoid any with soft or brown spots.

Store it: Eggplants are fairly delicate and should be used soon after purchasing them. You can store them at room temperature for a couple of days, but if you're planning to keep them longer, place in your refrigerator's vegetable drawer for no longer than a week.

Use it: If an eggplant is young, the skin is tender and can be eaten. If the eggplant is old (you know it's older if it's quite large), the skin may be tough and should be peeled. Older eggplants also become bitter and may require salting and rinsing before using. Young eggplants and varieties like Japanese and Italian eggplant are not bitter and don't require salting before using them. Eggplant can be roasted, sautéed, grilled, or broiled. Due to its spongy consistency, it soaks up oil very efficiently. To prevent your eggplant from becoming soggy and oily when frying it, make sure to coat it well in flour, egg, and breadcrumbs or panko first.

Tartine of Fresh Grilled Figs

SERVES 1

Dried figs are tasty and add texture to salads and baked goods, but a fresh fig is a thing of beauty. The soft skin and voluptuous shape are sexy enough, but then add the tender flesh, rich with subtle flavors of spice and jam, and you have something magical. When grilled, figs soften just enough to meld with goat cheese or any other type of cheese you like. If you're lucky enough to find fresh figs, this is an easy, no-fuss way to enjoy them. I created this recipe just for me, because my husband isn't a fan of fresh figs, but it can easily be doubled to serve two.

COOKING SPRAY, for the grill

2 fresh FIGS

1 teaspoon extra-virgin OLIVE OIL

1 slice SOURDOUGH BREAD

1½ tablespoons plain GOAT CHEESE

½ teaspoon fresh THYME leaves

½ teaspoon HONEY

¼ teaspoon aged BALSAMIC VINEGAR

1. Preheat a grill or a grill pan to medium-high. Coat with cooking spray.

2. If using a grill, you may wish to place the figs on a skewer or in a grill basket to prevent them from falling through the grate. Grill the figs for 3 minutes, turning halfway through, until tender. Transfer to a plate. Keep the grill or grill pan hot.

3. Brush the bread on both sides with the olive oil. Add the bread to the grill and grill for 30 seconds on each side. Spread the goat cheese over the grilled bread. Halve the figs and arrange them on top. Sprinkle the thyme leaves over the figs and drizzle with the honey and balsamic vinegar. Slice the tartine in half and gobble it up.

CALORIES 316

FAT 11.5g
sat 2.8g
mono 4.4g
poly 0.7g

PROTEIN 6g

CARBOHYDRATES 49g

FIBER 5g

CHOLESTEROL 41mg

IRON 0.8mg

SODIUM 243mg

POTASSIUM 305mg

CALCIUM 66mg

Twice-Baked Blues

SERVES 6

These little bursts of flavor are perfect for a game day party or any other gathering where you want to serve hearty finger food. You can make the elements in advance, wrap the unfilled potato halves and the filling separately, and then assemble and broil right before serving. Lots of people like the bite of blue-veined Gorgonzola cheese, but if you're not the biggest fan (like me), you can substitute feta.

1 pound (450g) small BLUE POTATOES

¼ teaspoon SALT

2 ounces (55g) GORGONZOLA DOLCE or FETA cheese

2 tablespoons 2% PLAIN GREEK YOGURT

1 tablespoon 2% MILK

2 teaspoons OLIVE OIL

1 SCALLION, the green part only, sliced

1. Preheat the oven to 350ºF (177ºC). Place potatoes on a rimmed baking sheet and bake for 35 minutes, until tender. Remove from the oven and let cool. Preheat the broiler to high.

2. Once the potatoes are cool enough to handle, cut them in half and scoop out the flesh with a melon baller or small spoon (be careful not to get too close to the skin). Transfer the flesh to a medium bowl and add the salt, cheese, yogurt, and milk, and mash with a large fork or potato masher.

3. Place the potato skins on the rimmed baking sheet. (To get the potato halves to sit upright, slice a bit off the bottoms with a knife.) Brush the potatoes with the oil and stuff each half with 1 to 2 teaspoons of the cheese filling, depending on the size of the potatoes.

4. Broil for 3 minutes, until slightly golden and heated through. Sprinkle with scallions and serve hot.

(per 2 halves)

CALORIES 105

FAT 4.8g
sat 2.3g
mono 1.2g
poly 0.2g

PROTEIN 4g

CARBOHYDRATES 13g

FIBER 1g

CHOLESTEROL 9mg

IRON 0.6mg

SODIUM 243mg

POTASSIUM 350mg

CALCIUM 65mg

Roasted Tricolor Carrots with Thyme

SERVES 8

Looking for a side dish that everyone will love? This simple preparation is always a crowd-pleaser and makes a great accompaniment to roast chicken or steak.

3 bunches purple, orange, and white BABY CARROTS (2½ pounds/1.1kg total), peeled or scrubbed, and stems trimmed to ¼ inch (6mm)

2 tablespoons OLIVE OIL

¼ teaspoon SALT

¼ teaspoon freshly ground BLACK PEPPER

2 teaspoons fresh THYME leaves

1. Preheat the oven to 400ºF (205ºC).

2. Place the carrots in a large baking dish. Drizzle them with the oil, and then sprinkle evenly with the salt, pepper, and thyme.

3. Roast for 40 minutes, turning the carrots halfway through, until they are tender. Serve.

CALORIES 80

FAT 3.7g
sat 0.5g
mono 2.5g
poly 0.6g

PROTEIN 1g

CARBOHYDRATES 12g

FIBER 4g

CHOLESTEROL 12mg

IRON 1.3mg

SODIUM 198mg

POTASSIUM 338mg

CALCIUM 47mg

Blue Potatoes/ Potatoes

RECIPES: **Roasted Fingerling Potato and Smoked Trout Salad,** page 122 **Late Summer Succotash,** page 126 **Twice-Baked Blues,** page 160

The basics: Like the tomato and eggplant, this tuber is part of the nightshade family and was once thought to be poisonous. The Europeans avoided it until the Irish demon-strated its versatility and healthfulness. Today, hundreds of varieties, including red, blue/purple, and gold potatoes, are grown throughout the world. Sizes range from large russet potatoes to the diminutive fingerling varieties.

Seasonality: Potatoes are available year-round. New potatoes are harvested from spring to early summer.

Good stuff: As their name suggests, potatoes are an excellent source of the electrolyte potassium, with 641mg per potato. They also have 2.5g of fiber and are a great source of resistant starch, which is a type of carbohydrate that acts like fiber and helps keep you feeling full longer. Blue/purple and red potatoes are an especially good source of anthocyanins, a type of plant pigment with antioxidant activity.

Pick it: Look for smooth, firm potatoes with no signs of cuts, bruises, sprouting, or green discoloration.

Store it: Potatoes are best when stored away from light, at temperatures between 45 and 55ºF (7 and 13ºC) in a well-ventilated place for up to two weeks. Refrigeration causes the potato's starch to convert to sugar, causing discoloration and a sweet taste. You can combat this effect by letting potatoes come to room temperature before cooking them. Do not rinse potatoes until you're ready to use them; dampness can lead to spoilage.

Use it: Rinse potatoes under running water and scrub them gently with a produce brush to remove any dirt. To get the greatest benefits, keep the skin on. Many of the nutrients in potatoes are water soluble, so boiling is not the healthiest method of cooking. Roasting, microwaving, and steaming are all good methods. The intense violet color of blue/purple potatoes makes them a gorgeous addition to salads. They are great in appetizer dishes as well. Try them roasted with other potatoes such as fingerlings and new potatoes.

Red Onions/ Onions

RECIPES: **Classic Marinara with Zucchini,** page 34 **Peperonata Bruschetta,** page 65 **Golden Gazpacho with Rock Shrimp,** page 67 **Red Lentil and Quinoa Cakes with Basil Cream,** page 79 **Glazed Red Cipollinis,** opposite **Caramelized Red Onion and Fig Pizza,** page 173

The basics: This pungent bulb is a native of ancient Palestine and central Asia. Along with garlic and leeks, onions are a member of the allium family. Depending on the variety, onions may either be relatively sweet or pack quite a punch. Red onions are fairly mild, as are Bermuda, Vidalia, Maui, and Spanish onions. Globe onions, which may have yellow, white, or red skin, have the strongest flavor. Onions also vary in size from tiny creamer or boiling varieties, such as pearl and cipollini onions, to Colossal and Super Colossal onions, which can be more than 4½ inches (11.5cm) in diameter.

Seasonality: Globe and red onions are available year-round. The varieties that hail from specific locations (Maui, Vidalia, Walla Walla) have more limited seasons.

Good stuff: A culinary powerhouse, the onion also offers a world of nutritional benefits. It is very high in polyphenols, including flavonoids, which are what give plants their color. Red onions have the highest levels of flavonoids, followed by yellow and white varieties. Quercetin is one of these flavonoids and has been found to have antioxidant and anti-inflammatory properties. Onions and other members of the allium family have sulfur-containing compounds in them, which is why they have such strong flavors and odors. These sulfur compounds have a variety of health properties, including anticancer and antimicrobial. Eating onions may also help prevent gastric ulcers by preventing the growth of the bacteria *H. pylori*.

Pick it: Onions should have smooth, dry skin and no sign of sprouting or mold.

Store it: Kept at room temperature with plenty of air circulation, onions will last for up to two months. To lessen their tear-inducing properties, you can store them in the refrigerator. Or place them in the fridge or freezer for 15 to 20 minutes before using them in a recipe. Once cut, an onion will keep tightly wrapped in the refrigerator for up to seven days.

Use it: There are countless ways to use an onion. Sliced raw, they make an excellent addition to sandwiches, burgers, and salads. When sautéed, they add depth of flavor to myriad dishes. Onions can also be roasted or glazed or used in slow-cooked dishes and soups. The smaller varieties lend themselves well to pickling.

Glazed Red Cipollinis

SERVES 6

I'm not going to lie—these little onions are a pain to peel. I know that I throw a few curse words around each time I make them. But the intensely earthy flavor you get is so worth it. And you can cook the dish up to two days before serving, making this the perfect make-ahead side dish for Thanksgiving or any holiday meal.

1 pound (450g) RED CIPOLLINI or PEARL ONIONS, unpeeled

⅓ cup (80ml) BALSAMIC VINEGAR, preferably aged

1 tablespoon DARK BROWN SUGAR

1 sprig fresh THYME

1 sprig fresh ROSEMARY

1 BAY LEAF

¼ teaspoon SALT

¼ teaspoon freshly ground BLACK PEPPER

½ tablespoon UNSALTED BUTTER

1. Preheat the oven to 400ºF (205ºC).

2. Bring a medium pot of water to a boil. Add the onions to the boiling water and cook for 1 minute. With a slotted spoon, transfer the onions to a bowl of cold water to stop the cooking process. When cool, peel the onions. Trim the ends if necessary.

3. In an ovenproof saucepan, combine the onions with the vinegar, brown sugar, thyme, rosemary, bay leaf, salt, and pepper. Bring to a simmer over medium-high heat and simmer for 2 minutes, moderating the heat as needed. Stir in the butter, then transfer to the oven.

4. Roast the onions for 25 minutes, stirring once halfway through. The onions will be glazed and tender.

CALORIES 57

FAT 1g
sat 0.6g
mono 0.3g
poly 0.04g

PROTEIN 1g

CARBOHYDRATES 11g

FIBER 2g

CHOLESTEROL 3mg

IRON 0.2mg

SODIUM 101mg

POTASSIUM 22mg

CALCIUM 7mg

Mom's Sweet-and-Sour Red Cabbage

SERVES 8

My mother grew up in Bad Nauheim, Germany, where she helped her parents with their inn and restaurant called Die Krone (The Crown). When I was growing up, she cooked several traditional German dishes, but one of the most memorable for me was her recipe for sweet-and-sour red cabbage. Though I was a pretty picky eater, I adored the cabbage and loved how it colored the mashed potatoes my mother would always serve with it. Mom never wrote the recipe down for me, but I reached out to German relatives and re-created it. I hope you enjoy it as much as I enjoyed taking the trip down memory lane. Grating the cabbage takes a while, so make sure to have some good tunes on!

1 medium head RED CABBAGE, tough outer leaves removed

¼ cup (60ml) OLIVE OIL

1 RED ONION, diced

2 FUJI APPLES, peeled, cored, and finely chopped

3 JUNIPER BERRIES

3 whole ALLSPICE BERRIES, or ¼ teaspoon ground allspice

3 whole CLOVES, or ¼ teaspoon ground cloves

1 BAY LEAF

½ teaspoon SALT

¼ teaspoon freshly ground BLACK PEPPER

3 tablespoons RED CURRANT JELLY

2 tablespoons BALSAMIC VINEGAR, preferably white

1 teaspoon LIGHT BROWN SUGAR

1. Using a box grater, mandoline, or a coarse Microplane grater, grate the cabbage. In a large saucepan, heat the oil over medium-high heat. Add the onion and sauté for 2 minutes.

2. Lower the heat to medium; add the cabbage and apples and stir to combine. Add the juniper berries, allspice berries, cloves, bay leaf, salt, pepper, jelly, vinegar, sugar, and ½ cup (120ml) of water and stir to combine. Turn the heat to low, cover, and cook for 40 minutes, until the cabbage is tender.

3. Remove the juniper berries, allspice berries, cloves, and bay leaf. Serve the cabbage hot or at room temperature. Refrigerate for up to 4 days. Leftovers can also be frozen in an airtight container for up to 1 month.

CALORIES 202

FAT 7.6g
sat 1.3g
mono 5.4g
poly 0.8g

PROTEIN 3.5g

CARBOHYDRATES 33g

FIBER 5g

CHOLESTEROL 0mg

IRON 1.2mg

SODIUM 180mg

POTASSIUM 472mg

CALCIUM 106mg

Rainbow Slaw

SERVES 6

My friend Esi was the inspiration behind this brightly hued salad made with red cabbage. She serves it with pulled pork, but I think it goes equally well with the Mushroom and Hominy Quesadillas on page 191. The slaw can be made one day before serving.

1 small head RED CABBAGE (about 1 pound/450g), shredded

1¼ cups (80g) CARROTS, shredded

1 RED or YELLOW BELL PEPPER, sliced thinly into strips and cut crosswise into 2-inch (5cm) pieces

1 cup (40g) fresh CILANTRO leaves, chopped

2 tablespoons APPLE CIDER VINEGAR

2 teaspoons extra-virgin OLIVE OIL

2 teaspoons whole-grain DIJON MUSTARD

1 tablespoon HONEY

3 tablespoons fresh ORANGE JUICE

¼ teaspoon SALT

¼ teaspoon freshly ground BLACK PEPPER

1. Toss the cabbage, carrots, bell pepper, and cilantro together in a large bowl.

2. In a small bowl, whisk together the vinegar, oil, mustard, honey, orange juice, salt, and pepper. Drizzle the vinaigrette over the vegetables and toss to combine. Cover and refrigerate until ready to serve.

CALORIES 60

FAT 1.8g
sat 0.2g
mono 1.2g
poly 0.2g

PROTEIN 1g

CARBOHYDRATES 11g

FIBER 2g

CHOLESTEROL 0mg

IRON 0.5mg

SODIUM 169mg

POTASSIUM 244mg

CALCIUM 32mg

Red Cabbage/ Cabbage

RECIPES: **Mustard-Crusted Pork Tenderloin with Napa Cabbage and Apple Slaw,** page 137 **Mom's Sweet-and-Sour Red Cabbage,** page 166 **Rainbow Slaw,** opposite **Gingered Salmon Over Black Rice with Bok Choy,** page 187

The basics: A member of the cruciferous family, cabbage may be either smooth or curly and ranges from white to green to deep purple-red.

Seasonality: Cabbage is available year-round.

Good stuff: Often an overlooked vegetable, cabbage has a wealth of nutritional benefits. It's high in fiber, low in calories (1 cup/89g raw has 22), has cholesterol-lowering attributes (when cooked), and is packed with cancer-fighting nutrients. Red cabbage in particular contains anthocyanin polyphenols, which give it its deep purple-red color. These pigments have anti-inflammatory properties.

Pick it: Choose a head of green or red cabbage with firm, tightly packed leaves. Savoy, Napa, and bok choy cabbages have more loosely packed leaves. No matter the variety, it should be heavy for its size. Avoid cabbage that looks dried out with cracked or wilted leaves. While convenient, precut cabbage and slaw has fewer nutrients than freshly cut cabbage.

Store it: Keep cabbage in the refrigerator, tightly wrapped, for up to one week.

Use it: Remove any damaged outer leaves and rinse well. You may want to halve the cabbage head and submerge it in water for 5 to 10 minutes to remove any possible sediment or critters. Cabbage is wonderful both raw and cooked. It can be shredded for slaw, tacos, and salads, and also grated. Cabbage is delicious braised and sautéed and can also be stuffed and steamed. It is also preserved to make sauerkraut and kimchi.

Plums

RECIPES: **Rhubarb-Plum Syrup,** page 37 **Oma's German Plum Cake,** opposite **Ultimate Power Balls,** page 204

The basics: Originally from China, plums are stone fruit and all varieties have firm flesh with a central pit. Though hundreds of varieties exist, there are two main categories: Japanese (which originate from China) and European. Japanese plums are larger and juicier and include the Santa Rosa variety. European plums are generally smaller and include damson plums.

Seasonality: Plums are in season from May through late October.

Good stuff: Diminutive in size, but big on flavor, plums are often overlooked for more traditional summer favorites. One plum has just 30 calories and is a good source of potassium. Dried plums (prunes) are renowned for helping with regularity, but the pectin they contain also helps keep your heart healthy by lowering both total and LDL (bad) cholesterol. Dried plums may also play a role in preventing osteoporosis.

Pick it: Look for plums that are firm, but not hard, and give to gentle pressure. Avoid those with brown spots—they have been damaged by the sun. The powdery-looking bloom that's on the surface of some plums is natural and actually indicates that the plum has not been handled too much.

Store it: Unripe plums can be kept at room temperature until ripe. Store ripe plums in the refrigerator for up to four days.

Use it: Plums make a refreshing snack and their sweet-tart flavor is a nice addition to salads and desserts. They can also be cooked and used in jams, sauces, and compotes. Fresh or dried, they go well with pork, game, and poultry.

Oma's German Plum Cake

SERVES 20

This is another recipe that required some sleuthing and cooperation from my German relatives. Plum cake is common throughout Germany and is called *zwetschgenkuchen*. It's said to have originated in the city of Augsburg, Bavaria. While not sweet in the traditional sense of "cake," this recipe is addictive nonetheless.

COOKING SPRAY, for the pan

¾ cup (90g) ALL-PURPOSE FLOUR

¾ cup (95g) WHOLE-WHEAT FLOUR

⅓ cup (65g) SUGAR

1 large EGG

1 cup (250ml) 2% MILK, at room temperature

¼ cup (½ stick/57g) UNSALTED BUTTER, at room temperature

Pinch of SALT

1 teaspoon pure VANILLA EXTRACT

1 (¼-ounce/7g) packet ACTIVE DRY YEAST

5 RED or BLACK PLUMS, pitted and cut into ¼-inch (6mm) slices

For the crumb topping:

½ cup (60g) ALL-PURPOSE FLOUR

¼ cup (50g) SUGAR

1 teaspoon pure VANILLA EXTRACT

½ teaspoon ground CINNAMON

¼ cup (½ stick/57g) UNSALTED BUTTER, softened

1. Preheat the oven to 350ºF (177ºC). Coat a 9-by-13-inch (23-by-33cm) baking pan with cooking spray and set aside.

2. Stir the flours and sugar together in the bowl of a stand mixer fitted with the flat beater attachment. Add the egg, milk, butter, salt, vanilla, and yeast. Mix on high speed for 5 minutes. Cover the bowl with a clean kitchen towel and leave on the counter, in a warm spot away from drafts, for 1 hour. The dough will double in size. Remove the dough from the bowl (it will be very sticky), transfer to a piece of plastic wrap, and refrigerate for 30 minutes.

3. Make the crumb topping: Place all of the ingredients into a small bowl. With clean hands, use your fingertips in a pinching motion to form crumbs. Set aside.

4. Remove the dough from the refrigerator and, with floured hands, press it into an even layer on the bottom of the prepared pan. Use a fork to prick the dough all over. Arrange the plum slices in rows, going lengthwise, in a slightly overlapping pattern.

5. Sprinkle the crumb topping all over the plums and bake for 30 to 35 minutes, until the crumbs and the edge of the crust are light golden. Let cool for 10 to 15 minutes, then cut into 20 squares and serve.

CALORIES 127

FAT 5.3g
sat 3.2g
mono 1.4g
poly 0.3g

PROTEIN 2.5g

CARBOHYDRATES 18g

FIBER 1g

CHOLESTEROL 22mg

IRON 0mg

SODIUM 39mg

POTASSIUM 80mg

CALCIUM 22mg

Caramelized Red Onion and Fig Pizza

MAKES ONE 10-INCH (25.5CM) PIZZA

Even people who love to cook have a secret fallback convenience food. Ours is the frozen caramelized onion and fig pizza from Fresh Direct, an online grocery delivery service in the New York area. My husband and I love it so much that I decided to re-create it. I think I've come pretty darn close, but if you've tried the one from Fresh Direct, I'd love to hear what you think. The recipe makes more caramelized onions than you'll need for the pizza, but they're really good, so I love having them around. Use them on salads, sandwiches, or for another pizza—they'll keep for three days in the refrigerator.

2 tablespoons extra-virgin OLIVE OIL

1 medium RED ONION, thinly sliced (see Note)

2 tablespoons BALSAMIC VINEGAR

¼ teaspoon SALT

¼ teaspoon freshly ground BLACK PEPPER

1 pound (450g) WHOLE-WHEAT PIZZA DOUGH, at room temperature

½ cup (about 2¾ ounces/75g) crumbled FETA CHEESE

4 ounces (115g) MOZZARELLA, shredded

½ cup (75g) dried MISSION FIGS, chopped

¼ cup (25g) WALNUTS, chopped

¼ teaspoon dried OREGANO

1. Preheat the oven to 500ºF (260ºC). Place a pizza stone or rimmed baking sheet in the oven.

2. In a sauté pan, heat the oil over medium heat. Add the onion and cook for 12 minutes, until translucent. Add the vinegar, salt, and pepper; stir and cook for 5 minutes more. Turn off the heat and set aside.

3. Roll out the dough between two pieces of parchment paper to a diameter of 10 inches (25.5cm). Remove the top sheet of parchment paper and cover the dough evenly with both cheeses, the figs and walnuts, half of the onions, and the oregano.

4. Reduce the oven temperature to 450ºF (232ºC) and transfer the pizza (on the parchment paper) to the pizza stone or baking sheet. Bake for 12 minutes, until the cheese is golden and the crust is crisp. Let rest for 5 minutes before slicing into 8 wedges and serving.

NOTE: If you have sensitive eyes like mine, try putting the red onion in the freezer for 15 to 20 minutes before slicing. It helps to cut down on the waterworks!

(per slice)

CALORIES 287

FAT 13g
sat 4g
mono 3.5g
poly 2.1g

PROTEIN 9g

CARBOHYDRATES 34g

FIBER 6g

CHOLESTEROL 20mg

IRON 0.4mg

SODIUM 508mg

POTASSIUM 112mg

CALCIUM 70mg

Roasted Red Grape and Mascarpone Parfait

SERVES 4

These incredibly rich parfaits make an easy year-round dessert or an elegant breakfast for guests. The salty-sweet combination elevates the grape from an everyday snacking fruit to the star of the show.

1 pound (450g) seedless RED GRAPES, washed and dried well (see Note)

½ teaspoon FLEUR DE SEL

½ cup (about 4 ounces/115g) MASCARPONE

¾ cup (175g) fat-free PLAIN GREEK YOGURT

2 teaspoons HONEY

1. Preheat the oven to 400ºF (205ºC).

2. Place the grapes on a rimmed baking sheet, sprinkle them with the salt, and roast for 15 minutes, until most of the grapes have burst and collapsed. Remove from the oven.

3. While the grapes roast, combine the mascarpone and yogurt in a medium bowl.

4. Spoon ¼ cup (60ml) of the yogurt mixture into each of 4 parfait or wine glasses. Top each with ⅓ cup (40g) of the grapes, and another ¼ cup (60ml) of the yogurt mixture. Drizzle each with ½ teaspoon of the honey and serve.

NOTE: Make sure the grapes are completely dry before roasting them. If they are still wet, the moisture will cause them to steam instead of roast. Yuck!

CALORIES 234

FAT 13.3g
sat 7.2g
mono 0.01g
poly 0.05g

PROTEIN 7g

CARBOHYDRATES 25g

FIBER 1g

CHOLESTEROL 35mg

IRON 0.4mg

SODIUM 383mg

POTASSIUM 217mg

CALCIUM 80mg

Grapes

The basics: Grown in temperate climates all over the world, grapes are berries that grow in bunches on vines. There are thousands of varieties, ranging from green to red to black. In the United States, grapes were first planted by Spanish friars next to the California missions they built. The term "table grapes" refers to the low-acid varieties that we eat. Wine grapes are too acidic to enjoy as a snack, but make wonderful wines.

Seasonality: California grows 98 percent of the grapes grown in the United States. Their season runs from May through January. You can find imported grapes throughout the year.

Good stuff: Grapes (including green, red, and black) contain a mix of antioxidants, including flavonoids and resveratrol. Resveratrol has anti-inflammatory properties and is a potent antioxidant. Resveratrol shows promise in helping to combat a range of maladies, from Alzheimer's and Parkinson's diseases to cancer to aging. Grapes also play a role in heart health, promoting healthy arteries, improving blood flow, and helping to keep platelets from sticking together, which can lead to the formation of clots.

Pick it: Look for plump grapes with no spots or wrinkles. The berries should be firmly attached to their stems.

Store it: Store grapes in a plastic bag in the refrigerator for up to a week. Wash them thoroughly just before serving. While some people like to bring grapes to room temperature to enjoy their full flavor, others prefer eating them chilled or even frozen.

Use it: Of course, grapes make a wonderful, healthy snack. But they can also be used in a range of sweet and savory recipes. Sliced or halved, grapes make a juicy addition to salads and grain dishes. They also bring sweetness to salsas and other sauces. Roasting brings out the deep, plumlike flavor in grapes, which lets them pair well with creamy items including cheese, ice cream, and yogurt.

Blacks & Tans

While perhaps not colorful in the traditional sense, the foods that fall into this family have just as much to boast about as their flashier counterparts. Rich in fiber and antioxidants, these whole grains, legumes, fruits, fungi, and seeds add big flavor and texture to meals and reduce your risk of diabetes and heart disease. And let's not forget that chocolate falls into this group!

Pumpkin Seed-Chia Granola with Mango

MAKES 6 CUPS (750G)

I'm a sucker for good granola. But so much of the stuff you find at the market is either loaded up with extra oil and sugar or is incredibly expensive. While making granola is slightly time-consuming, it is really easy. And this recipe yields a hearty amount, so you'll be able to enjoy it for several breakfasts. It also makes a welcome housewarming gift.

COOKING SPRAY, for the pan (if needed)

2 cups (310g) old-fashioned ROLLED OATS

½ cup (120g) CHIA SEEDS

½ cup (70g) shelled raw PUMPKIN SEEDS

1 cup (200g) diced dried MANGO

¼ cup (25g) dried BLUEBERRIES

½ cup (25g) flaked unsweetened COCONUT

¼ teaspoon ground CINNAMON

Pinch of SALT

3 tablespoons UNSALTED BUTTER, melted

2 tablespoons CANOLA OIL

½ cup (125ml) HONEY

1. Preheat the oven to 350ºF (177ºC). Place a silicone mat on a rimmed baking sheet or spray a rimmed baking sheet with cooking spray.

2. In a large bowl, mix together the oats, chia seeds, pumpkin seeds, mango, blueberries, coconut, cinnamon, and salt. In another bowl, combine the butter, oil, and honey. Pour the wet ingredients over the dry, stir to combine, and spread the mixture onto the prepared baking sheet in an even layer.

3. Bake the granola for 20 minutes, until golden. Let cool for at least 15 minutes, then use your hands to break the granola into pieces. Transfer to an airtight container (I like lidded glass jars). The granola will stay fresh for 1 week to 10 days.

(per ¼ cup)

CALORIES 136

FAT 6.6g
sat 2.4g
mono 1.8g
poly 2g

PROTEIN 3g

CARBOHYDRATES 18g

FIBER 3g

CHOLESTEROL 4mg

IRON 1mg

SODIUM 10mg

POTASSIUM 50mg

CALCIUM 35mg

Mohonk Mountain Muesli

MAKES 3 CUPS (495G)

Our family spends time at the Mohonk Mountain House in the Catskills each summer. One of the most delicious items on the breakfast buffet is the muesli. It's great for fueling morning hikes. Here's my version of it. Try any dried fruit you like in the mix. The muesli will keep in an airtight container for up to a month.

For the muesli:

2 cups (310g) old-fashioned ROLLED OATS (see Note)

¼ cup (60g) FLAXSEED

¼ cup (60g) HEMP SEEDS

½ cup (65g) dried APRICOTS, sliced

¼ cup (60ml) MILK, or non-dairy alternative

½ teaspoon pure MAPLE SYRUP

Nut and Fruit Toppings:

1 tablespoon sliced ALMONDS

⅓ cup (40g) GRAPES, halved

Or

1 tablespoon chopped WALNUTS

½ medium BANANA, sliced

1. Make the muesli: Place the oats, flaxseed, hemp seeds, and apricots in a bowl. Mix well and transfer to a jar or other airtight container.

2. To serve, place ½ cup of the muesli in a bowl and add the milk and maple syrup. Cover and refrigerate for at least 2 hours or overnight. Stir and top with your choice of nuts and fruit.

NOTE: If you follow a gluten-free diet, you can make this with certified gluten-free oats, like those from Bob's Red Mill.

WITH ALMONDS AND GRAPES:

CALORIES 311

FAT 10.7g
sat 1.8g
mono 2.8g
poly 1.4g

PROTEIN 1.3g

CARBOHYDRATES 24g

FIBER 5g

CHOLESTEROL 5mg

IRON 3mg

SODIUM 29mg

POTASSIUM 527mg

CALCIUM 127mg

WITH WALNUTS AND BANANAS:

CALORIES 367

FAT 12.7g
sat 1.9g
mono 2.2g
poly 3.5g

PROTEIN 12g

CARBOHYDRATES 54g

FIBER 9g

CHOLESTEROL 5mg

IRON 4mg

SODIUM 29mg

POTASSIUM 717mg

CALCIUM 116mg

Oats

The basics: This popular whole grain is originally from Asia. Oats come in several varieties ranging from the least processed and healthiest Irish or "steel-cut" oats to instant oats, which are partially boiled, dried, and rolled very thinly. Irish oats can take 40 minutes to cook, while instant oats can simply be stirred together with boiling water to make a hot breakfast cereal. Rolled oats are made from hulled grains that are steamed and then rolled. Oat bran is the outer casing of the grain and is very high in fiber. You can also buy oat flour, which is essentially just ground oats. You can make oat flour by pulsing rolled oats in your food processor.

Seasonality: All varieties of oats can be purchased year-round.

Good stuff: Mom was right—you should eat your oatmeal. Long touted for their cholesterol-lowering effects, oats have an extensive list of benefits. Oats help you feel full; they also aid in lowering blood pressure, may help reduce the risk of type 2 diabetes, and improve insulin sensitivity. What's so magical about the lowly oat? Most of the benefits appear to be related to the beta-glucan content. Beta-glucan is the soluble fiber in oats.

Pick it: Most recipes call for rolled oats, but make sure to read carefully to be sure. Depending on the texture you like, you might prefer rolled oats or steel-cut oats for breakfast cereal. Instant oats are certainly the most convenient, and these days you can even buy microwavable steel-cut oats.

Store it: Oats should be stored in an airtight container in a cool, dry pantry for up to six months. You can also store them for up to a year in the freezer.

Use it: Wonderful as a hot morning meal, oats can also be used in desserts and baked goods including bread, cobblers, and crumbles. And steel-cut and rolled oats make tasty sides such as salads with dried fruit and nuts, as well as stuffing. They can also up the health quotient in meatloaf, meatballs, and casseroles.

Chia Seeds

RECIPES: **Spice Girl Pumpkin Muffins,** page 56 **Matcha Panna Cotta,** page 146 **Pumpkin Seed–Chia Granola with Mango,** page 178

The basics: Chia seeds were a staple of the Aztec and Mayan diets and were prized for their ability to provide long-lasting energy. Chia comes from the *Salvia hispanica* plant, which is in the mint family and is native to Mexico and Guatemala.

Seasonality: Chia seeds can be purchased year-round.

Good stuff: Chia contains alpha-linolenic acid (ALA), which is a type of omega-3 fatty acid found in plant foods. ALA has anti-inflammatory benefits. Chia seeds are also high in fiber, gluten-free, and a good source of protein.

Pick it: Chia seeds are now being used in energy bars, beverages, and snack foods, though the whole seed may still be a challenge to find at the supermarket. You can find it online and at health food stores.

Store it: You can store chia seeds in an airtight container in a cool dry place or keep them in the refrigerator for longer storage. Discard when they're past their expiration date.

Use it: Chia is incredibly versatile, and thanks to the tiny size of the seed, they are quite inconspicuous. You can sprinkle the seeds over cereal and yogurt, or add them to smoothies and even soups. To make a "chia gel" to use as a thickener in creamy soups, simply combine ¼ cup (42g) chia seeds with 2 cups (480ml) of water, let stand for 15 to 30 minutes, and then stir with a whisk. The gel can also be added to fruit juice or coconut milk to make a vegan pudding or mixed with mashed fresh fruit to make a jam.

Hemp Seeds

RECIPE: **Mohonk Mountain Muesli**, page 180

The basics: Often misunderstood, hemp has a rich history. Hemp has long been used to make ropes, sails, cloth, oil, and paper. In fact, the Declaration of Independence was drafted on paper made from hemp. Its flavor is nutty and slightly grassy.

Seasonality: Hemp products can be purchased year-round.

Good stuff: The hemp plant is great for the planet as well as your body. It requires no pesticides or herbicides to grow and uses very little water. It is a cousin of the marijuana plant, but it does not contain any THC. What it does boast are high levels of ALA omega-3 and omega-6 fatty acids, fiber, protein, and essential amino acids.

Pick it: Hemp may be purchased as a powder, as an oil, or as the whole hulled seed.

Store it: Due to its high (healthy) fat content, store hemp products in the refrigerator or freezer and discard them when they're past their expiration date.

Use it: The whole seeds can be sprinkled over cereal, salads, or yogurt, or added to baked goods. The oil can't be used for cooking, but it's great for making salad dressings and for drizzling over roasted vegetables and pasta dishes. Hemp powder can be used in smoothies.

Barley

RECIPES: **Italian Barley Salad with Herb Oil,** page 125 **Sweet or Savory Breakfast Barley,** opposite

The basics: A whole grain, barley has been grown since the Stone Age. In addition to being used in cereals and bread, barley is used in animal feed and is also fermented to make whiskey and beer.

Seasonality: Dried barley is available year-round. It's found packaged in boxes, as well as in the bulk section of health food stores.

Good stuff: Barley has a wonderful chewiness and a subtle nutty flavor. Of all the whole grains, barley is highest in fiber. One type of fiber it contains, beta-glucan, helps reduce LDL (bad) cholesterol, stabilize blood sugar, and boost immune system function. Barley is also rich in resistant starch, a type of carbohydrate that acts like fiber and helps keep you feeling full longer.

Pick it: Barley has a hard, inedible husk, which must be removed, or hulled, before the grain can be used. If the bran of the grain is also removed, it's referred to as "pearl" or "pearled" barley. While still healthy, it doesn't have as much fiber as when the bran is left intact, but it does take a bit less time to cook. I prefer to use hulled barley, which still has the bran.

Store it: Barley is best stored in an airtight container in the freezer for up to a year. Though it takes at least 40 minutes to cook, plain cooked barley can be stored in the refrigerator for up to a week, or frozen in a zip-top bag or container for up to a month.

Use it: Much like rice, barley can be used in salads, as a side dish, and also as a breakfast cereal. You can also add it to soups and use barley flour in breads and other baked goods.

Sweet or Savory Breakfast Barley

SERVES 6

This recipe is like a choose-your-own adventure story, which I loved when I was a kid. Once you've cooked the barley, you can take it in a sweet direction or go savory. Either way, it's the perfect thing to prep and then take to work or school. Barley is mega high in fiber (11g per cup!) and contains resistant starch, which means it will keep you feeling full for hours.

For the barley:

2 cups (368g) uncooked hulled BARLEY, rinsed

Pinch of SALT

For the sweet version, per serving:

2 tablespoons unsweetened ALMOND MILK or other milk

¼ teaspoon ground CINNAMON

1 teaspoon HONEY

⅛ teaspoon pure VANILLA EXTRACT

1 tablespoon GOLDEN RAISINS

1 small PEAR, such as Forelle, chopped

1 tablespoon chopped WALNUTS

For the savory version, per serving:

COOKING SPRAY, for the pan

1 large EGG

⅛ teaspoon SALT

⅛ teaspoon freshly ground BLACK PEPPER

1 teaspoon SRIRACHA HOT CHILI SAUCE

½ teaspoon grated PARMESAN

3 CHERRY TOMATOES, halved

1. Cook the barley: In a large saucepan, combine the barley with the salt and 5 cups (1.1L) of water and bring to a boil. Reduce the heat to medium-low and simmer, uncovered, for 40 minutes, until tender but still chewy. Drain off any excess water.

2. Once the barley is cooked, you may use it immediately to create a sweet or savory breakfast or let it cool and transfer it to a large container. It will keep in the refrigerator for up to 1 week. When you're ready to enjoy it, just choose one of the following methods:

• To make the sweet version: Place 1 cup (225g) of cooked barley in a microwave-safe bowl. Whisk the milk, cinnamon, honey, vanilla, and raisins together in a small bowl and then pour over the barley. Microwave for 40 seconds. Place the pear and walnuts on top.

• To make the savory version: Place 1 cup (225g) of cooked barley in a microwave-safe bowl. Spray a small sauté pan with cooking spray and heat over high heat. Add the egg, sprinkle with the salt and pepper, and cook for 2 minutes, until the white has set and the yolk is still wobbly. Heat the barley for 40 seconds in the microwave, then place the egg on top. Drizzle with the Sriracha and sprinkle the cheese on top. Serve the cherry tomatoes on the side.

SWEET:

CALORIES 411

FAT 0.29g
sat 0.03g
mono 0.03g
poly 0.1g

PROTEIN 10g

CARBOHYDRATES 83g

FIBER 17g

CHOLESTEROL 0mg

IRON 3mg

SODIUM 59mg

POTASSIUM 593mg

CALCIUM 84mg

SAVORY:

CALORIES 300

FAT 6.3g
sat 1.9g
mono 2g
poly 1.7g

PROTEIN 15g

CARBOHYDRATES 48g

FIBER 11g

CHOLESTEROL 186mg

IRON 3mg

SODIUM 59mg

POTASSIUM 499mg

CALCIUM 61mg

Gingered Salmon over Black Rice with Bok Choy

SERVES 2

Like brown rice, black rice is rich in antioxidants and fiber. Most of the benefits are housed in the outer layer of bran that covers the grain. That bran makes black rice take a while to cook, but its rich, nutty flavor is worth it. And it's pretty gorgeous, too, especially with salmon.

1 cup (200g) BLACK JAPONICA RICE

Pinch of SALT

1 tablespoon low-sodium SOY SAUCE

2 tablespoons grated fresh GINGER

2 teaspoons pure MAPLE SYRUP

2 teaspoons seasoned RICE VINEGAR

2 teaspoons MIRIN

1½ teaspoons OLIVE OIL

1 SHALLOT, minced

2 heads BABY BOK CHOY, halved

1 teaspoon CANOLA OIL

2 (6-ounce/170g) SALMON FILLETS, preferably wild

1 teaspoon BLACK SESAME SEEDS

2 teaspoons chopped SCALLIONS

1. Bring the rice, salt, and 2 cups (500ml) of water to a boil in a medium saucepan over high heat. Reduce the heat to low and simmer, covered, for 40 to 45 minutes, until the water is completely absorbed. Fluff and set aside.

2. In a small bowl, whisk together the soy sauce, ginger, maple syrup, vinegar, and mirin. Set aside.

3. When the rice has about 15 minutes left to cook, prepare the bok choy. In a large sauté pan, heat the olive oil over medium-high heat and add the shallot. Cook for 1 minute, reduce the heat to medium, and add the bok choy. Cook for 2 minutes per side. Transfer the bok choy and shallot to a plate and keep warm. Wipe the pan clean with paper towels.

4. In the same sauté pan, heat the canola oil over medium-high heat and add the salmon. Pour half of the soy-ginger mixture into the pan and cook the salmon for 4 minutes per side. Transfer the cooked salmon to the plate with the reserved bok choy. Add the remaining soy-ginger mixture to the pan and warm over medium heat.

5. Onto each of 2 dinner plates, place 1 cup of rice. Top the rice with a salmon fillet and serve 2 bok choy halves alongside. Sprinkle each fillet with ½ teaspoon of the sesame seeds and 1 teaspoon of the scallions. Drizzle half of the warmed soy-ginger sauce over each plate, and serve hot.

CALORIES 535

FAT 18g
sat 3.3g
mono 8g
poly 5.5g

PROTEIN 43g

CARBOHYDRATES 52g

FIBER 5g

CHOLESTEROL 90mg

IRON 2mg

SODIUM 602mg

POTASSIUM 702mg

CALCIUM 57mg

Black Bean, Corn, Green Grape, and Avocado Salad

SERVES 6

I have made so many variations of this salad, depending on what I have on hand at the time. I find that kids love it—even if they pick out some of the things they don't like. Willa loves black beans and grapes, so this recipe gets her to experiment with other foods she's not a huge fan of.

1 teaspoon finely grated LIME ZEST

2 tablespoons fresh LIME JUICE

¼ teaspoon SALT

¼ teaspoon ground CAYENNE PEPPER

1 (15-ounce/425g) can low-sodium BLACK BEANS, rinsed and drained

1 ripe but firm MANGO, peeled, pitted, and diced (see page 59)

1 ripe but firm AVOCADO, pitted, peeled, and diced

¼ cup (10g) fresh CILANTRO leaves

1 ear CORN, cooked and kernels removed

½ JALAPEÑO PEPPER, seeded and minced

½ cup (55g) GREEN GRAPES, quartered

1. In a small bowl, combine the lime zest and juice, salt, and cayenne pepper. Add the beans to the lime mixture and stir to coat evenly.

2. In a large bowl, gently toss together the mango, avocado, cilantro, corn, jalapeño, and grapes. Add the black beans and gently toss to combine. Serve at room temperature or chill for 1 hour before serving.

CALORIES 158

FAT 5.5g
sat 0.9g
mono 3.5g
poly 0.8g

PROTEIN 5g

CARBOHYDRATES 28g

FIBER 7g

CHOLESTEROL 0mg

IRON 1.5mg

SODIUM 249mg

POTASSIUM 557mg

CALCIUM 36mg

Black Rice

RECIPE: **Gingered Salmon over Black Rice with Bok Choy,** page 187

The basics: Also known as "forbidden" rice, black rice was considered the finest grain in ancient China and was only served to the emperor. It turns a deep purple color when cooked.

Seasonality: Black rice can be purchased year-round.

Good stuff: Its rich, nutty flavor isn't the only thing that black rice has going for it. Studies have found that black rice and black rice bran contain anthocyanins, a type of antioxidant, at levels similar to blueberries and blackberries. Anthocyanins may play a role in cancer and heart disease prevention. Black rice appears to have an anti-inflammatory effect, and may be useful in preventing and treating dermatitis and other inflammatory conditions. Additionally, black rice contains minerals including iron, magnesium, and manganese.

Pick it: While growing in popularity, black rice can still be difficult to find at grocery stores. Look for it in health food stores or order it online. (See Resources, page 214.)

Store it: Keep black rice in an airtight bag or container in a cool, dark place for six months or in the freezer for up to a year.

Use it: Try black rice in recipes where you usually use brown rice or wild rice. Mix it with quinoa for a pilaf. And it makes a stunning rice pudding when cooked with coconut milk.

Black Beans

RECIPES: **Tortilla Soup with Homemade Chips,** page 95 **Black Bean, Corn, Green Grape, and Avocado Salad,** page 188 **Mushroom and Hominy Quesadillas,** opposite

The basics: Also known as turtle beans, these small beans are popular in Central and South America, the Caribbean, Mexico, and the southern United States.

Seasonality: Black beans can be purchased dried and in cans year-round.

Good stuff: With a slightly sweet flavor and great texture, black beans work well in a variety of dishes. They're also super high in fiber, with 15g per cup (240g), making them a smart food for diabetics and anyone trying to lose weight. They're also packed with iron, potassium, and folate.

Pick it: Look for black beans that are not faded. A faded color indicates that the beans were stored in sunlight and may become rancid more quickly. Canned beans are generally salted, but you can now find beans canned with no added salt. It's smarter to buy them this way and add salt to suit your taste.

Store it: Dried beans can be stored in a bag or an airtight container away from light for up to one year. Canned beans last even longer, but make sure to look at the expiration date on the can.

Use it: Dried beans need to be soaked prior to cooking. Use 3 cups (720ml) of water for every 1 cup (204g) of dried beans. Soak the beans overnight, then drain and rinse them with clean water. Add the beans to a pot with enough water to cover them. Simmer for 2 to 4 hours until beans are tender. If using canned beans, make sure to rinse them well before using them. Not only will this significantly reduce the sodium in beans canned with salt, it will also cut down on the gas-producing oligosaccharides (a type of carbohydrate).

Whether you're working with dried or canned beans, they can be used in a wide range of dishes from burritos and dip to salads and soup. You can even use mashed black beans in brownies. They add moisture and body, helping to replace some or all of the flour in gluten-free recipes, and of course they boost the fiber, too. And you'll really never know they're in there!

Mushroom and Hominy Quesadillas

SERVES 4

Quesadillas are a quick weeknight dinner or lunch, and using mushrooms makes this version perfect for Meatless Mondays. I love the addition of the chewy hominy, but if you can't find it, you can also use corn. The quesadillas go well with my Rainbow Slaw (page 168).

1 tablespoon plus 2 teaspoons extra-virgin OLIVE OIL

1 SHALLOT, minced

1 small JALAPEÑO PEPPER, seeded and minced (optional)

8 ounces (225g) baby PORTOBELLO MUSHROOMS, sliced

¼ teaspoon SALT, plus a pinch more

¼ teaspoon freshly ground BLACK PEPPER

1 (15-ounce/425g) can low-sodium BLACK BEANS, rinsed and drained

1 (15-ounce/425g) can WHITE HOMINY, rinsed and drained

1 ripe AVOCADO, pitted and peeled

Juice of 1 LIME

4 (8-inch/20cm) WHOLE-GRAIN TORTILLAS

4 ounces FONTINA CHEESE, grated (see Note)

1. Heat 1 tablespoon olive oil in a large sauté pan over high heat. Add the shallot. Turn the heat down to medium-high and cook for 1 minute, until golden. Add the jalapeño and mushrooms, season with ⅛ teaspoon each of salt and pepper, and sauté, stirring frequently, for 5 minutes. Transfer to a bowl.

2. Add the remaining 2 teaspoons oil to the same pan, return to medium-high heat, and add the beans and hominy. Season with the remaining ⅛ teaspoon salt and pepper and cook for 3 minutes. Transfer the beans and hominy to the bowl with the mushrooms and mash the mixture lightly with a potato masher or large fork.

3. In a small bowl, mash the avocado with the lime juice. Season with a pinch of salt.

4. Wipe out the pan with a paper towel. Place a tortilla in the pan and spread with ¼ of the mashed avocado, then top with 1 cup (186g) of the mushroom-bean mixture, and sprinkle with ¼ cup (25g) of cheese. Heat over medium-high heat for 3 minutes, then fold the tortilla in half over the filling and gently press down with a spatula. Heat for another 3 to 4 minutes, until cheese is melted. Transfer to a cutting board and cover with foil to keep warm. Repeat with the remaining tortillas and filling, then cut each of the cooked quesadillas into 4 wedges and serve.

NOTE: Put the fontina in the freezer for 5 minutes before grating it. It can be a challenge to shred at room temperature.

CALORIES 492

FAT 25g
sat 7g
mono 11g
poly 2g

PROTEIN 26g

CARBOHYDRATES 58g

FIBER 24g

CHOLESTEROL 33mg

IRON 2mg

SODIUM 815mg

POTASSIUM 737mg

CALCIUM 217mg

Roast Mushrooms with Wine Reduction over Couscous

SERVES 5

People don't eat enough mushrooms. Maybe it's their color—or lack thereof. Or maybe it's a texture issue. I like their woodsy appeal. If you've never been a fan, give this recipe a try. And enjoy a glass of the Cabernet while you're waiting for the wine in the pan to reduce.

8 ounces (225g) MUSHROOMS (combination of oyster, shiitake, and baby portobello), sliced

¼ teaspoon SALT

¼ teaspoon freshly ground BLACK PEPPER

8 sprigs fresh THYME

1 large clove GARLIC, sliced

2 tablespoons extra-virgin OLIVE OIL

1 SHALLOT, minced

2 cups (500ml) CABERNET SAUVIGNON

1 cup (175g) uncooked COUSCOUS

1 cup (250ml) boiling WATER

¼ cup (25g) grated PARMESAN, plus more for serving

2 tablespoons chopped fresh flat-leaf PARSLEY leaves

1. Preheat the oven to 350°F (177°C).

2. In a roasting pan, arrange the mushrooms in 1 layer. Sprinkle with the salt and pepper, add 5 sprigs of the thyme and the garlic, and drizzle with 1 tablespoon of the oil. Roast for 25 minutes, until tender.

3. While the mushrooms are roasting, heat the remaining 1 tablespoon olive oil in a small saucepan over high heat. Add the shallot and cook for 1 minute. Add the wine and remaining 3 sprigs thyme, reduce the heat to medium-high, and simmer for 30 minutes, until reduced by half.

4. When there are about 10 minutes remaining on the reduction, place the couscous in a medium-size heatproof bowl. Add the boiling water to the couscous, let sit for 5 minutes, then fluff with a fork. Stir in the cheese and fluff again.

5. Divide the couscous among 5 serving bowls. Top each with 3 tablespoons (37g) of the roasted mushrooms, about 1½ tablespoons of the reduction, and about 1 teaspoon of the parsley. Serve with extra grated Parmesan on the side.

CALORIES 301

FAT 7.6g
sat 1.7g
mono 4g
poly 0.9g

PROTEIN 8g

CARBOHYDRATES 34g

FIBER 3g

CHOLESTEROL 4mg

IRON 1mg

SODIUM 248mg

POTASSIUM 267mg

CALCIUM 101mg

Mushrooms

RECIPES: **Mushroom and Hominy Quesadillas,** page 191 **Roast Mushrooms with Wine Reduction over Couscous,** opposite

The basics: Mushrooms were first cultivated in France and came to the United States in the late nineteenth century. Cultivated mushrooms are grown in climate-controlled rooms in specially formulated compost. Mushrooms don't contain chlorophyll, so they need to receive all of their nutrients from the compost they grow in.

Seasonality: Several mushroom varieties are grown indoors year-round. They include button, cremini, shiitake, maitake, enoki, beech, and oyster. Wild mushrooms grow at various times of the year. Unless you are harvesting them with someone extremely knowledgeable, it's not advisable to pick and eat wild mushrooms. Enjoy them at a reputable restaurant instead!

Good stuff: Mushrooms are magical indeed. With their umami characteristics, they have the ability to channel the deep flavors of meat and are often used in dishes that typically call for meat. And while they hardly contain any calories—five medium mushrooms have 20 calories—they have plenty of hidden talents. Mushrooms are among the few foods that contain significant amounts of vitamin D, which is important for building and maintaining strong bones because it helps the body absorb calcium. Vitamin D appears to play a role in other conditions including preeclampsia, cardiovascular disease, diabetes, impaired immune function, and cancer. The recommended daily intake for vitamin D is 600 IU (International Units). Most mushrooms contain between 1 and 6 percent of the daily value for vitamin D, but maitake mushrooms offer up a whopping 236 percent! Mushrooms are also a leading source of selenium, a mineral with antioxidant properties.

Pick it: Mushrooms should have smooth, dry skin with no dark spots.

Store it: Keep mushrooms in their original packaging or in a paper bag in the refrigerator. They should last for up to a week. Fresh mushrooms shouldn't be frozen, but cooked mushrooms can be frozen for up to a month.

Use it: Clean mushrooms with damp paper towels, or rinse them briefly under running water and dry them gently with a paper towel. Don't soak mushrooms in water—they'll drink up all the moisture and become mushy. Trim woody stems. Stems should be removed completely from shiitake mushrooms. Mushrooms are wonderful sautéed, stuffed, or stir-fried. Large mushrooms, like portobellos, can be grilled. Some mushroom varieties, like enoki and button, can be used raw.

Freekeh

The basics: The word actually refers to any grain that is harvested and roasted when it's still young and green. The freekeh that you can find on the market now is wheat. The flavor is similar to regular bulgur wheat, but it's grassier and a little softer once cooked. Freekeh is brownish-green.

Seasonality: Freekeh can be purchased year-round.

Good stuff: With a nutty flavor and a chewy consistency, freekeh is similar to other grains like barley. Some people also describe its flavor as smoky. Because freekeh is harvested when it's young, the grain retains more nutrition, providing more protein, fiber, and minerals than in wheat harvested when it's mature. It also ranks low on the glycemic index.

Pick it: Freekeh is available whole and cracked. You can find it at health food stores, but it's still making its way into the American marketplace, so you may need to purchase it online (see Resources, page 214).

Store it: Keep freekeh in a cool, dry place and use by the expiration date on its original package.

Use it: Freekeh cooks in about 20 minutes and can be used in place of brown rice and barley in various dishes. It's a nice addition to pilafs, soups, stews, and salads.

Freekeh Tabbouleh

SERVES 6

I'm a fan of tabbouleh, but I've had my share of disappointing experiences with it. While it's a simple dish, there seem to be many ways to go wrong with its assembly. You want it to be flecked with fresh mint and parsley, but the ratio of herbs to grain shouldn't be overpowering. The salad should be nice and light, but skip the oil completely and you'll end up with a dry, cough-inducing dish. I think this version is quite balanced and the freekeh gives it a nice twist. If you can't find freekeh, you can make the recipe with bulgur wheat.

2 cups (363g) cracked FREEKEH

½ teaspoon KOSHER SALT

¼ cup (60ml) fresh LEMON JUICE (from 1½ lemons)

2 tablespoons extra-virgin OLIVE OIL

¼ teaspoon SALT

¼ teaspoon freshly ground BLACK PEPPER

¼ cup (5g) fresh flat-leaf PARSLEY leaves, chopped

¼ cup (10g) fresh MINT leaves, chopped

1 medium hothouse CUCUMBER, quartered and sliced into pieces

1. In a large saucepan, bring the freekeh, salt, and 5 cups (1.1L) of water to a boil. Turn down to a simmer and cook, covered, for 20 minutes, until all of the water has been absorbed. Remove from the heat and allow to cool. Once it has cooled, transfer the freekeh to a large bowl.

2. In a small bowl, whisk the lemon juice, oil, salt, and pepper together. Drizzle the mixture over the freekeh. Add parsley, mint, and cucumber and stir well to combine. Serve immediately or refrigerate in an airtight container for up to 5 days.

CALORIES 253

FAT 5.4g
sat 0.7g
mono 3.6g
poly 0.4g

PROTEIN 6g

CARBOHYDRATES 45g

FIBER 6g

CHOLESTEROL 0mg

IRON 2mg

SODIUM 259mg

POTASSIUM 32mg

CALCIUM 13mg

Yogurt Parfait with Maple Freekeh

SERVES 4

To me there's nothing prettier than a parfait for breakfast, lunch, or a substantial afternoon snack. I once had a yogurt parfait with wheat berries in it, which inspired me to get creative with freekeh. When combined with the creamy yogurt, it adds a wonderful chewiness that I find addictive. Feel free to play around with seasonal fruits and other types of nuts.

1 cup (182g) uncooked WHOLE-GRAIN FREEKEH

1 tablespoon pure MAPLE SYRUP

1¼ cups (300g) low-fat VANILLA YOGURT

1 APPLE, such as Fuji or Lady Apple, cored and chopped (1¾ cups/200g)

3 tablespoons shelled PISTACHIOS, chopped

4 STRAWBERRIES, hulled and sliced

1. Combine the freekeh with 3 cups (750ml) of water in a saucepan and bring to a boil. Boil for 35 minutes, until the grain is tender but not mushy. Allow the freekeh to cool slightly, then transfer 1 cup (160g) to a bowl and reserve the rest for another use.

2. To the freekeh in the bowl, add the maple syrup and stir. Set aside.

3. In each of 4 pretty glasses, spoon 2 tablespoons of the maple freekeh. Top with 2 tablespoons yogurt, then 3 tablespoons of the apple, 1 teaspoon chopped pistachios, 2 tablespoons freekeh, 3 tablespoons yogurt, then ¼ cup (25 grams) apple, and about 1¼ teaspoons pistachios. Top with 1 sliced strawberry.

CALORIES 261

FAT 3g
sat 1g
mono 1g
poly 0.6g

PROTEIN 8g

CARBOHYDRATES 50g

FIBER 6g

CHOLESTEROL 5mg

IRON 1mg

SODIUM 51mg

POTASSIUM 126mg

CALCIUM 124mg

Flaxseed

RECIPES: **Spice Girl Pumpkin Muffins**, page 56 **Mohonk Mountain Muesli**, page 180 **Stout Bread with Chocolate**, page 210

The basics: Cultivated since Babylonian times, flaxseed is used to make linseed oil. It's mainly known for its health properties. Today flaxseed is grown primarily in Canada.

Seasonality: Flaxseed and ground flaxseed can be purchased year-round.

Good stuff: Usually touted for its high ALA omega-3 content, flaxseed has other healthy attributes as well. It is very high in lignans, which act as antioxidants. The ALAs, along with the lignans, contribute to its anticancer benefits by helping to block the enzymes that are involved with making hormones that promote the growth of certain cancers. Flaxseed also helps keep your heart healthy by lowering blood pressure and bad cholesterol, and by helping to keep arteries clear. Are you running to the store to buy some yet? Go!

What Are Lignans?

There are high amounts of lignans in both flaxseed and sesame seeds. Lignans are also found in broccoli, cabbage, soybeans, oats, wheat, rye, and barley, and also apricots and strawberries. Lignans are complex carbohydrates (fiber) that when digested act as phytoestrogens. Phytoestrogens are plant compounds that work like estrogen in the body, helping to lower cholesterol; they may also help relieve the symptoms of menopause, including hot flashes. (Research on the benefits of phytoestrogens is ongoing.)

Pick it: Depending on how you plan to use it, you can choose either whole or ground flaxseed. It is available in brown and golden varieties. Both are equally healthy, but the golden variety is slightly sweeter.

Store it: Due to its high (healthy) fat content, flaxseed and ground flaxseed should be kept in a closed container in the refrigerator or freezer for up to six months.

Use it: Adding whole flaxseed to oatmeal and baked goods will add fiber plus a pleasant crunch and a nutty flavor. But the seeds likely won't break down during the digestive process, so you won't get the omega-3 benefit. To tap into that, grind the seeds before adding them to your recipes. You can use a coffee or spice grinder to grind them yourself, or buy the seeds already ground.

You can substitute ground flaxseed in baked goods for one-quarter to one-half of the amount of flour called for in the recipe. You can also add ground flaxseed to meatballs, smoothies, and chili.

Press-to Pesto Picnic Sandwich

SERVES 4

I learned this brick-pressed sandwich technique from Martha Stewart's *Living* magazine about fifteen years ago. It's a brilliant approach to sandwiches for a picnic or an evening concert under the stars. Assemble the sandwich about 4 to 6 hours before you plan to eat it and it will be perfect.

1 small EGGPLANT (10 ounces/280g), sliced

¼ teaspoon SALT

1 tablespoon OLIVE OIL, plus more for the grill

1 (1-pound/450g) WHOLE-WHEAT RUSTIC BREAD round, such as a boule

4 ounces (115g) plain GOAT CHEESE, at room temperature

2 tablespoons PARSLEY PESTO (page 91) or store-bought pesto

10 marinated OLIVES, pitted and halved

1. Preheat a grill to medium-heat or a grill pan over medium-high heat.

2. Salt the eggplant on both sides and let it sit on paper towels for 15 minutes to allow any liquid to be absorbed. Press it with a clean paper towel to absorb any remaining moisture. Brush the eggplant on both sides with the olive oil and transfer to a plate.

3. When you're ready to grill, oil the grill or grill pan. Add the eggplant and grill for 5 minutes per side, until tender. Transfer to a plate and set aside.

4. Cut the round of bread in half horizontally. Remove and discard some of the soft interior of the bread. Spread the goat cheese over the bottom half of the bread, then top with the pesto. Arrange about 6 eggplant slices over the pesto (keep the remaining eggplant for another use), then add the olives.

5. Place the top part of the bread over the olive layer and wrap the sandwich completely in parchment paper. Tie with string or ribbon, whatever you have that's handy. Place the wrapped sandwich in the refrigerator and top with either 2 heavy, large books (this one would work!) or a clean brick or heavy pan. Remove the sandwich after 4 to 6 hours, cut it into 4 pieces, and serve.

CALORIES 392

FAT 23g
sat 7.3g
mono 6.3g
poly 1g

PROTEIN 11g

CARBOHYDRATES 35g

FIBER 4g

CHOLESTEROL 73mg

IRON 1mg

SODIUM 773mg

POTASSIUM 208mg

CALCIUM 113mg

Olive-Fig Tapenade

MAKES 1¾ CUPS TAPENADE (350ML); 14 SERVINGS

I love the versatility of olive tapenade. You can simply spread it over toasted baguette or crackers, or you can use it as a sandwich spread or as a topping for roasted fish. It's excellent when combined with goat cheese, especially this version with its secret ingredient of dried figs. I added the figs to boost the fiber of the tapenade, and also to give it a bit of sweetness to balance out the salty bite of the olives and capers. Give it a try, but if you're really opposed to the figs, leave them out.

1½ cups (218g) pitted KALAMATA OLIVES, rinsed and drained

2 tablespoons CAPERS, rinsed and drained

4 DRIED FIGS (3½ ounces/100g), sliced

1 teaspoon grated LEMON zest

1 tablespoon fresh LEMON juice

1 teaspoon grated ORANGE zest

1 tablespoon fresh ORANGE juice

¼ cup (5g) fresh flat-leaf PARSLEY leaves

2 tablespoons extra-virgin OLIVE OIL

Combine all the ingredients except the olive oil in a food processor. Pulse a few times, scrape down the sides, then add the oil and pulse a few more times. The tapenade should not be entirely smooth, and should still have some texture to it. Store in an airtight container in the refrigerator for up to 1 week.

CALORIES 72

FAT 6g
sat 1g
mono 5g
poly 0.7g

PROTEIN 0.4g

CARBOHYDRATES 4g

FIBER 0.5g

CHOLESTEROL 0mg

IRON 0.3mg

SODIUM 301mg

POTASSIUM 29mg

CALCIUM 12mg

Olives

RECIPES: **Panzanella Niçoise Salad**, page 121 **Italian Barley Salad with Herb Oil**, page 125 **Press-to Pesto Picnic Sandwich**, page 199 **Olive-Fig Tapenade**, opposite

The basics: Olives were first cultivated in Crete and Syria five thousand years ago. Prized for their oil, olives are a fruit that grow on the olive tree. They flourish in warm climates, including Tunisia, Morocco, Spain, and California. Fresh olives are bitter, and the final flavor depends on when the olive is picked and what process it goes through before it's eaten. Unripe olives are always green, but ripe olives can be black, purple, brown, or green (red olives are colored with food dye). There are hundreds of olive varieties, including manzanilla, kalamata, niçoise, sevillano, and picholine.

Seasonality: Olives are harvested in September and are available year-round in various preparations.

Good stuff: Salty, meaty, and incredibly delicious, olives are prized for their flavor as well as their oil and are a staple of the Mediterranean diet. The fat found in olives is three-quarters heart-healthy monounsaturated fat. Increasing monounsaturated fat in the diet helps to lower total cholesterol, LDL (bad) cholesterol, and improve the LDL:HDL ratio. The monounsaturated fat in olives can also help lower blood pressure. Olives also contain various types of phytonutrients, which have both antioxidant and anti-inflammatory properties. Olive polyphenols have been shown to lower blood levels of C-reactive protein, which is a marker for determining the likelihood of inflammation in the body. And while they do contain a high percentage of (good) fat, each large olive is just 5 calories. Bargain!

Pick it: Olives can be purchased pitted or unpitted, stuffed or unstuffed, marinated or plain. Olives may be oil-cured, water-cured, brine-cured, dry-cured, or lye-cured.

Store it: Canned olives can be stored in a cool, dark place for up to a year. Once opened, transfer the olives to an airtight container, cover with the canning brine, refrigerate, and use within two weeks. Olives purchased from an olive bar should be stored in an airtight container in the refrigerator for up to 1 week.

Use it: Olives make a wonderful addition to a cheese plate, tapas platter, or any appetizer presentation. They're also delicious in salads, omelets, tapenades, and a variety of Mediterranean-inspired dishes.

Quinoa

RECIPES: **Cherry Tomato, Sausage, and Quinoa Tart,** page 48 **Red Lentil and Quinoa Cakes with Basil Cream,** page 79 **Quinoa Biscotti with Currants, Cherries, and Almonds,** opposite

The basics: Usually thought of as a grain, quinoa is actually an edible seed. It grows on magenta stalks 3 to 9 feet (1 to 2.75m) tall. Quinoa was considered sacred by the Incas, who referred to it as the "mother of all grains." Quinoa is related to beets, chard, and spinach, and the leaves of the plant can be eaten as a vegetable.

Seasonality: Since it's purchased dried in boxes or in bulk, you can find quinoa products year-round.

Good stuff: This versatile, quick-cooking pseudo-grain is nutty, delicious, and a smart food for vegetarians and meat eaters alike. It's one of the few plant foods that provide a complete protein, and it's also high in heart-healthy potassium, immune-boosting zinc, and all-important iron. Quinoa is gluten-free.

Pick it: There are red, white, and black varieties of quinoa. You can also purchase it as a blend. Quinoa flakes and flour are also sold. You can also buy sprouted quinoa, which removes the bitter saponins found naturally on the seeds. I prefer to use the sprouted kind because I don't need to soak it, and the sprouting process also appears to improve the digestibility and enhance the nutritional benefits of quinoa. (For information on sprouted quinoa, see Resources on page 214.)

Store it: Keep quinoa in an airtight container for up to four months. Store the container on a cool, dry pantry shelf. You can also keep it in the freezer for up to eight months. If the grains give off a musty or oily smell, they are past their prime.

Use it: If you're not using sprouted quinoa, give it a quick rinse to remove any bitter saponin residue. In a medium saucepan, bring 1½ cups (360ml) of water to a boil, then add 1 cup (175g) of dried quinoa. Reduce the heat to a simmer, cover, and cook for 12 to 15 minutes, or until the water is absorbed. Let the quinoa sit for 5 minutes, then fluff with a fork. I like to cook at least 1 cup (175g) of dry quinoa at a time, which makes 3 cups (365g) cooked quinoa. You can make less, but I find that it gets used up pretty fast! Once cooked, you can use it as a side dish, in baked goods, salads, patties, soups, and more.

Quinoa Biscotti with Currants, Cherries, and Almonds

MAKES ABOUT 22 BISCOTTI

It's so nice to have a treat on hand that can go with morning coffee or an afternoon cup of green tea. These biscotti are wonderful because they remain a bit soft, unlike traditional biscotti. My son, Leo, loves to munch on them. These untraditional biscotti are also gluten-free.

1¾ cups (193g) QUINOA FLOUR (see Note)

1 cup (200g) SUGAR

2 teaspoons BAKING POWDER

½ teaspoon SALT

¾ teaspoon ground CINNAMON

3 large EGGS

¼ cup (60ml) CANOLA OIL

1 teaspoon ORANGE ZEST

1 tablespoon fresh ORANGE JUICE

¾ teaspoon pure VANILLA EXTRACT

¾ cup RAW ALMONDS, toasted and coarsely chopped

½ cup (65g) dried CURRANTS

½ cup (70g) dried CHERRIES

1. Preheat the oven to 350ºF (177ºC). Place a Silpat mat or sheet of parchment paper on a baking sheet, or coat with cooking spray; set aside.

2. In a large bowl, stir together the flour, sugar, baking powder, salt, and cinnamon.

3. In a medium bowl, whisk together the eggs, oil, orange zest, juice, and vanilla. Add the wet ingredients to the dry and combine. Stir in the almonds, currants, and cherries.

4. Separate the dough into two halves and with clean hands, form each dough half into an 8-inch (20cm) long loaf on the prepared baking sheet. Bake for 25 minutes, or until lightly golden. Let cool for 20 minutes on the baking sheet, then transfer to a cutting board and slice crosswise into ½-inch wide (1.25cm) cookies (about 11 per loaf). Using a spatula, carefully transfer the biscotti back onto the baking sheet (cut side down) and bake again for 14 minutes, until the tops are dry to the touch and the biscotti are hard nearly all the way through. The cookies will further harden as they continue to cool.

NOTE: Quinoa flour is simply ground quinoa. It is more perishable than regular wheat flour and should be stored in the refrigerator or freezer.

(per biscotti)

CALORIES 141

FAT 6g
sat 0.6g
mono 3g
poly 1.4g

PROTEIN 3g

CARBOHYDRATES 19g

FIBER 3g

CHOLESTEROL 25mg

IRON 1mg

SODIUM 115mg

POTASSIUM 74mg

CALCIUM 34mg

Ultimate Power Balls

MAKES ABOUT 25 BALLS

Before morning runs, I'm always looking around the kitchen for a healthy nibble that will hold me over until I can eat a proper breakfast. These 86-calorie bites are just the ticket. And since they are dairy- and nut-free (and wheat-free if you use puffed rice), they pass the school test!

½ cup (10g) PUFFED MILLET

1 cup (20g) PUFFED KAMUT or PUFFED RICE

½ cup (90g) diced DRIED PLUMS (prunes; see Note)

⅓ cup (60g) SEMISWEET CHOCOLATE CHIPS

¼ cup (35g) SESAME SEEDS

⅓ cup (80g) SUNFLOWER BUTTER, at room temperature

½ cup (125ml) HONEY

¾ cup (40g) shredded unsweetened COCONUT

1. In a large bowl, toss together the puffed millet and puffed kamut or rice. Add the dried plums, chocolate chips, and sesame seeds.

2. Stir in the sunflower butter and the honey. You should have a nice sticky mess! Cover the bowl with plastic wrap and refrigerate for 30 minutes.

3. Place the coconut in a small bowl. Using a tablespoon, scoop the mixture and form it into 1-inch (2.5cm) balls with your hands. Roll the balls in the coconut and transfer to a container. You can store the power balls in the refrigerator for up to 1 week, or in the freezer in a zip-top freezer bag for up to 1 month, but I bet they won't last that long!

NOTE: There's a product from Sunsweet called Plum Amazins that is essentially just diced dried plums. Since they can be annoyingly sticky to chop up, I find the prediced ones helpful for putting this recipe together quickly.

(per power ball)

CALORIES 86

FAT 4.9g
sat 2g
mono 1.9g
poly 0.7g

PROTEIN 1.4g

CARBOHYDRATES 24g

FIBER 1g

CHOLESTEROL 0mg

IRON 0.6mg

SODIUM 13mg

POTASSIUM 72mg

CALCIUM 19mg

Sesame Seeds

RECIPES: **Gingered Salmon over Black Rice with Bok Choy,** page 187 **Ultimate Power Balls,** page 204

The basics: Sesame seeds are found in the pods of the sesame plant, which is native to Indonesia and eastern Africa. It was brought to the United States by African slaves, who called it benne seed. Nutty-tasting sesame seeds can either be cream-colored, black, yellow, or red. They are used as a topping on bagels, breads, and desserts, as a seasoning in many cuisines, and also to make a tahini paste and a rich Middle Eastern dessert called halvah.

Seasonality: You can find sesame seeds year-round.

Good stuff: Sesame seeds are a surprisingly good source of calcium. A 1-ounce (28g) serving has 280mg of calcium, or as much as 8 ounces (245g) of yogurt. They're also a great source of vegetarian iron, as well as magnesium. Sesame seeds also contain high amounts of lignans. (To learn more about lignans, turn to page 197).

Pick it: Sesame seeds are sold in jars and also in bulk. It's better to buy the seeds in a container with an expiration date on it because they are very perishable.

Store it: Sesame seeds have a very high oil content, so they become rancid fairly quickly. You can store them in an airtight container at room temperature for three months, in the refrigerator for six months, or in the freezer for a year.

Use it: The sweet, nutty flavor of sesame seeds makes them incredibly versatile. They add crunch and texture to baked goods and are a wonderful finish to stir-fries and other Asian dishes. And of course sesame paste—tahini—is a vital component of hummus. You can make your own tahini by first lightly roasting (but not browning) 4 cups (575g) of seeds, then processing them with ¼ cup (60ml) of vegetable oil to make a paste. You can store the paste in the refrigerator for a few months.

Coconut

The basics: Coconuts are grown on coconut palm trees, which are found in Malaysia, Southwest Asia, India, Hawaii, and the Pacific Islands. The coconut fruit has a rough hairy husk and contains both white coconut meat ("copra") and water. Coconut milk is made from cooking the crushed or shredded meat with water. Dried coconut flakes or shredded coconut, both sweetened and unsweetened, are other coconut products.

Seasonality: Coconuts grow year-round, but the season peaks from October through December.

Good stuff: After being on the bad list for years, coconut is experiencing a renaissance. Coconut water is touted for its rich electrolyte content, which makes it suitable as a post-exercise drink. Coconut oil was once shunned due to its high saturated fat content, but there is evidence that the particular type of saturated fat it contains (medium-chain triglycerides or MCTs) does not raise overall cholesterol levels, only good HDL cholesterol. It's still not a license to load up your meals with lots of coconut oil and coconut milk, but coconut products can definitely be part of a healthy diet.

Pick it: If you're buying a whole coconut, look for one that is heavy for its size and sounds like it has lots of liquid inside when shaken. The three coconut "eyes" should be dry, not damp, and the shell should be free of cracks. When shopping for other coconut products, make sure to read the label carefully. For example, cream of coconut is often confused with coconut milk. The former is a blend of coconut paste, water, and sugar and is used to make piña coladas, while the latter is unsweetened and is used in curries and other savory dishes.

Store it: A whole unopened coconut can be kept at room temperature for up to six months. Shredded coconut should be stored in the freezer due to its high fat content.

Use it: To get the coconut water from a fresh coconut, carefully pierce the coconut's eyes with an ice pick or other sharp implement. Drain the water into a container and then proceed to hit the coconut with a hammer all around the perimeter. The coconut should crack open, allowing you to remove the flesh. There are plenty of tools available to make the process of removing the coconut meat somewhat easier. And of course, dried shredded coconut and frozen grated coconut (Birds Eye and other companies make it) is readily available at most grocery stores, as well as coconut water, milk, and butter, which is spreadable coconut meat. Try using shredded coconut in muffins and other baked goods. Coconut milk is wonderful in Indian curries, braises, and soups. Coconut water ups the nutrition in smoothies and is great on its own as a refreshing drink.

Nutty Chocolate Bark

SERVES 12

You might have to kick everyone out of the house when you make this recipe. The aroma of melting chocolate is usually too much for my husband to bear, and I find him circling me in the kitchen, hoping I'll let him lick a spatula or catch a few dribbles from the pot. This bark is easy to make, but looks quite impressive. Make a double batch for a neighbor or your tough-to-please mother-in-law.

9½ ounces (270g) SEMISWEET CHOCOLATE (see Note)

¼ cup (28g) shelled unsalted PISTACHIOS, chopped

¼ cup (38g) HAZELNUTS, chopped

½ cup (100g) dried CHERRIES, chopped

3 tablespoons flaked unsweetened COCONUT

¼ teaspoon coarse SEA SALT

1. Place water in the bottom of a double boiler and bring to a boil. (If you don't have a double boiler, place a heatproof bowl over a saucepan of gently simmering water, making sure the bottom of the bowl isn't touching the water.) Meanwhile, chop the chocolate into large chunks. Set aside 1 tablespoon each of the pistachios, hazelnuts, cherries, and coconut to top the chocolate. Place a Silpat mat or sheet of parchment paper on a rimmed baking sheet; set aside.

2. Melt the chocolate in the top of the double boiler, stirring occasionally. Once the chocolate is completely melted and smooth, turn off the heat and stir in the pistachios, hazelnuts, cherries, and coconut. Pour the chocolate mixture onto the prepared baking sheet, spreading it out with a spatula to an approximately 8-by-10-inch (20-by-25.5cm) rectangle. Sprinkle the reserved 1 tablespoon each of pistachios, hazelnuts, cherries, and coconut evenly on top. Sprinkle the salt evenly over the chocolate.

3. Transfer the baking sheet to the freezer and freeze for 1 hour, until completely firm. Using your hands, break the chocolate into chunks and enjoy, or transfer to a sealed container. Store in the freezer for best results.

NOTE: I like to use Scharffen Berger semisweet baking chocolate (62 percent cacao), which comes in a 9.7-ounce (275g) bar, but any semisweet bar will do. If you do get the Scharffen Berger, go ahead and use the entire bar. A wee bit of extra chocolate never hurt anyone!

CALORIES 162

FAT 12g
sat 6.3g
mono 1.7g
poly 0.6g

PROTEIN 3g

CARBOHYDRATES 17g

FIBER 4g

CHOLESTEROL 0mg

IRON 1mg

SODIUM 59mg

POTASSIUM 49mg

CALCIUM 8mg

Stout Bread with Chocolate

MAKES ONE 9-BY-5-INCH (23 BY 12.75CM) LOAF; SERVES 10

I've always found the idea of stout appealing—it looks so chocolatey and rich. But after a few sips, I feel full and the booze goes right to my head. As an ingredient in baking, however, I've found it gives an amazing flavor boost with its deep, bitter notes. This bread is not too sweet and is wonderful slathered with a layer of almond butter.

1 cup (120g) ALL-PURPOSE FLOUR

½ cup (62g) WHOLE-WHEAT FLOUR

¼ teaspoon SALT

1 teaspoon BAKING SODA

1 tablespoon ground FLAXSEED

½ cup (100g) DARK BROWN SUGAR

½ teaspoon ground CINNAMON

½ cup (125ml) STOUT (see Note)

½ cup (125g) WHOLE MILK VANILLA YOGURT

1 large EGG, whisked

2 tablespoons UNSALTED BUTTER, melted

1 teaspoon pure VANILLA EXTRACT

⅓ cup (54g) SEMISWEET CHOCOLATE CHUNKS or CHIPS

COOKING SPRAY, for the pan

1. Preheat the oven to 350°F (177°C).

2. Combine the flours, salt, baking soda, flaxseed, sugar, and cinnamon in a large bowl. Combine the stout, yogurt, egg, butter, and vanilla in another bowl. Make a well in the center of the dry ingredients and add the wet ingredients. Combine with a spatula, then stir in the chocolate.

3. Spray a 9-by-5-inch (23-by-12.75cm) loaf pan with cooking spray, then pour in the bread mixture. Bake for 40 minutes, until the top of the loaf feels dry and a sharp knife inserted into the middle comes out clean. Let cool for 10 to 15 minutes in the pan, then remove the loaf from the pan and slice into 10 pieces.

NOTE: You can use any stout in this recipe, but I love using a local brew called Brooklyn Brewery Black Chocolate Stout. It imparts an even richer flavor than a typical stout. It's only available from October through March, so stock up when you find it.

CALORIES 180

FAT 5.5g
sat 3.2g
mono 1.0g
poly 0.6g

PROTEIN 4g

CARBOHYDRATES 29g

FIBER 2g

CHOLESTEROL 26mg

IRON 0.7g

SODIUM 201mg

POTASSIUM 78mg

CALCIUM 33mg

Chocolate

The basics: Chocolate comes from the cacao tree, which grows on farms in tropical areas in West Africa, South and Central America, and Southeast Asia. The cacao bean grows inside a pod on the tree. Once harvested, cacao beans are fermented and dried. Then they travel to a factory, where they are cleaned and roasted. The part of the bean that is used to make the chocolate we eat is the meat inside, which is referred to as the nib. To remove the nib, the beans need to be cracked. The nibs are then ground into chocolate liquor. It does not contain any alcohol, it's simply liquid chocolate. The liquor is then poured into molds and hardened, resulting in unsweetened chocolate, which is then made into the various chocolate products we use.

Seasonality: Happily, chocolate can be found all year-round.

Good stuff: Rich in heart-protective flavonols, dark chocolate has been shown to help lower blood pressure, reducing the risk of stroke and heart disease. It may also aid in keeping your skin hydrated and your brain sharp. Chocolate contains the bone-building minerals magnesium, manganese, copper, zinc, and phosphorus (in small amounts). All the more reason to indulge your sweet tooth! While chocolate does contain some saturated fat, it is mostly stearic acid, and unlike most saturated fats, does not increase cholesterol levels.

Pick it: Though I admit to indulging in milk chocolate now and again, the healthiest option for snacking are bars made with at least 70 percent cacao. The higher the percentage, the less added sugar is in the chocolate. However, the percentage of cacao is not an indicator of how much flavonol the chocolate contains. How the beans are processed and stored and how the chocolate is handled all affect the flavonol content of the finished product. For baking it's best to go with a semisweet chocolate.

Store it: Store chocolate, tightly wrapped, in a cool, dry place (60 to 70ºF / 15 to 21ºC). I actually keep my chocolate in the freezer and bring it to room temperature before eating it or using it in recipes. If chocolate is stored in warm conditions, the cocoa butter will rise to the surface and form a "bloom," or slight whitening of the chocolate. The chocolate is still safe to eat, but the quality and flavor may be affected.

Use it: I don't think you need much help with this one! In addition to snacking on chocolate, it is of course wonderful in baked goods, beverages, and desserts. Unsweetened cocoa powder and Mexican chocolate (a mixture of chocolate, cinnamon, almonds, and vanilla) can also be used in savory sauces, including mole.

SOURCES

REDS

STRAWBERRIES
California Strawberry Commission (calstrawberry.com); Driscoll's (driscolls.com)

POMEGRANATES
Langley, Patricia, "Why a pomegranate?", *British Medical Journal* v.321(1153), Nov 4, 2000; *The New Food Lover's Companion* (Barron's, 2007); POM Wonderful (pomwonderful.com); WebMD (webmd.com)

WATERMELON
Cancer.org; *The New Food Lover's Companion* (Barron's, 2007); University of Kentucky Cooperative Extension Service (http://ces.ca.uky.edu/ces/)

RADICCHIO
Ninfali, P., et al., "Antioxidant capacity of vegetables, spices and dressings relevant to nutrition," *British Journal of Nutrition* 93 (2005): 257–266; *The New Food Lover's Companion* (Barron's, 2007); Royal Rose (radicchio.com); USDA National Nutrient Database; *The Visual Food Lover's Guide* (Wiley, 2009)

BEETS
The New Food Lover's Companion (Barron's, 2007); *The Visual Food Lover's Guide* (Wiley, 2009)

TOMATOES
Cancer.org; Melissa's (melissas.com); *The New Food Lover's Companion* (Barron's, 2007);

RADISHES
Melissa's (melissas.com); *The New Food Lover's Companion* (Barron's, 2007)

RHUBARB
Melissa's (melissas.com); *The New Food Lover's Companion* (Barron's, 2007); *The Visual Food Lover's Guide* (Wiley, 2009); USDA National Nutrient Database

CRANBERRIES
The New Food Lover's Companion (Barron's, 2007); Ocean Spray (cranberryhealth.com); Bodet, C., et al., "Potential oral health benefits of cranberry," *Critical Reviews in Food Science and Nutrition* 48 (2008): 672–80

RASPBERRIES
Driscoll's (driscolls.com); *The New Food Lover's Companion* (Barron's, 2007); *The Visual Food Lover's Guide* (Wiley, 2009)

APPLES
The New Food Lover's Companion (Barron's, 2007); U.S. Apple Association (usapple.org); *The Visual Food Lover's Guide* (Wiley, 2009)

CHERRIES
The Cherry Marketing Institute (choosecherries.com); Howatson, G., et al., "Effect of tart cherry juice (Prunus cerasus) on melatonin levels and enhanced sleep quality," *European Journal of Nutrition* 51 (2012): 909–16; National Cherry Growers & Industries Foundation (www.nationalcherries.com/health.html); *The New Food Lover's Companion* (Barron's, 2007); USDA National Nutrient Database

ORANGES

MANGOS
The National Mango Board (mango.org); *The New Food Lover's Companion* (Barron's, 2007)

ORANGES
Melissa's (melissas.com); *The New Food Lover's Companion* (Barron's, 2007)

APRICOTS
Melissa's (melissas.com); *The New Food Lover's Companion* (Barron's, 2007); *The Visual Food Lover's Guide* (Wiley, 2009); Whitehead, R. D., et al., "You Are What You Eat: Within-Subject Increases in Fruit and Vegetable Consumption Confer Beneficial Skin-Color Changes," PLoS ONE 7(2012): e32988, doi:10.1371/journal.pone.0032988

CANTALOUPE
Melissa's (melissas.com); *The New Food Lover's Companion* (Barron's, 2007); *The Visual Food Lover's Guide* (Wiley, 2009)

BUTTERNUT SQUASH
American Heart Association (heart.org); Melissa's (melissas.com)

PEACHES
The New Food Lover's Companion (Barron's, 2007); Mayo Clinic (mayoclinic.com); "The Health Benefits of Peaches," *The Saturday Evening Post*, saturdayeveningpost.com/2012/08/16/health-and-family/medical-update/peaches.html

SWEET POTATOES
The North Carolina Sweet Potato Commission (www.ncsweetpotatoes.com)

PUMPKINS
Melissa's (melissas.com); *The New Food Lover's Companion* (Barron's, 2007)

YELLOWS

STAR FRUIT
The American Optometric Association (aoa.org); Melissa's (melissas.com); *The Visual Food Lover's Guide* (Wiley, 2009)

FIGS
California Fig Advisory Board (californiafigs.com); Vinson, et al., "Dried Fruits: Excellent in vitro and in vivo antioxidants," *Journal of the American College of Nutrition* 24 (2005): 44–50; *The New Food Lover's Companion* (Barron's, 2007)

LEMONS
Linus Pauling Institute (http://lpi.oregonstate.edu/); Melissa's (melissas.com); WebMD (webmd.com); USDA National Nutrient Database; Dhanavade, et al., "Study Antimicrobial Activity of Lemon (*Citrus lemon* L.) Peel Extract," *British Journal of Pharmacology and Toxicology* 2(3): 119–122, August 5, 2011

BELL PEPPERS
Melissa's (melissas.com); *The New Food Lover's Companion* (Barron's, 2007); Office of Dietary Supplements, National Institutes of Health (http://ods.od.nih.gov/)

GREENS

ASPARAGUS
The New Food Lover's Companion (Barron's, 2007); *The Visual Food Lover's Guide* (Wiley, 2009); USDA National Nutrient Database

MUSTARD GREENS
Institute of Medicine, Dietary Reference Intakes (iom.edu/Activities/Nutrition/SummaryDRIs/DRI-Tables.aspx); *The New Food Lover's Companion* (Barron's, 2007); USDA National Nutrient Database

FENNEL
The New Food Lover's Companion (Barron's, 2007); *The Visual Food Lover's Guide* (Wiley, 2009)

KALE
Eco Localizer (ecolocalizer.com); Melissa's (melissas.com); *The New Food Lover's Companion* (Barron's, 2007)

WATERCRESS
Linus Pauling Institute (http://lpi.oregonstate.edu/); *The New Food Lover's Companion* (Barron's, 2007); USDA National Nutrient Database; Lind, "Watercress: Legendary Harbinger of Spring," *Edible Madison*, Spring 2011, ediblemadison.com/articles/view/watercress-legendary-harbinger-of-spring/c/full/

BRUSSELS SPROUTS
Linus Pauling Institute (http://lpi.oregonstate.edu/); *The New Food Lover's Companion* (Barron's, 2007); Melissa's (melissas.com)

BROCCOLI
Linus Pauling Institute (http://lpi.oregonstate.edu/); *The New Food Lover's Companion* (Barron's, 2007); Cramer and Jeffery, "Sulforaphane Absorption and Excretion Following Ingestion of a Semi-Purified Broccoli Powder Rich in Glucoraphanin and Broccoli Sprouts in Healthy Men," *Nutrition and Cancer Journal* v.63(2): 196–201, January 13, 2011, USDA National Nutrient Database

AVOCADOS
California Avocado Commission (californiaavocado.com); *The New Food Lover's Companion* (Barron's, 2007); USDA National Nutrient Database

SPINACH
The New Food Lover's Companion (Barron's, 2007); USDA National Nutrient Database

HERBS (rosemary, mint, parsley, tarragon, basil, dill, cilantro)
The New Food Lover's Companion (Barron's, 2007); Zheng and Wang, "Antioxidant Activity and Phenolic Compounds in Selected Herbs," *Journal of Agricultural and Food Chemistry* v49(11): 5165–5170, September 28, 2001

SUGAR SNAP PEAS
The New Food Lover's Companion (Barron's, 2007); USDA National Nutrient Database

ZUCCHINI
The George Mateljan Foundation (whfoods.com); *The New Food Lover's Companion* (Barron's, 2007); University of Minnesota Extension (www.extension.umn.edu); USDA National Nutrient Database

EDAMAME
Soyfoods Association of North America (soyfoods.org)

CUCUMBERS
The New Food Lover's Companion (Barron's, 2007); Melissa's (melissas.com); Kentucky Cooperative Extension Service (ca/uky.edu/CES); USDA National Nutrient Database

ARUGULA
USDA National Nutrient Database; *The Visual Food Lover's Guide* (Wiley, 2009)

LIME
The New Food Lover's Companion (Barron's, 2007); *The Visual Food Lover's Guide* (Wiley, 2009); USDA National Nutrient Database

BLUES, INDIGOS & VIOLETS

BLUEBERRIES
Lau, F.C., et al., "The Beneficial Effects of Fruit Polyphenols on Brain Aging," *Neurobiology of Aging* Suppl 1 (2005): 128–32; Cassidy, A., et al., "High Anthocyanin Intake is Associated with a Reduced Risk of Myocardial Infarction in Young and Middle-Aged Women," *Circulation* 127 (2013): 188–196; *The New Food Lover's Companion* (Barron's, 2007); *The Visual Food Lover's Guide* (Wiley, 2007); The U.S. Highbush Blueberry Council (blueberrycouncil.org)

BLUE POTATOES/POTATOES
United States Potato Board (www.potatogoodness.com); USDA National Nutrient Database

RED ONIONS/ONIONS
Melissa's (melissas.com); *The New Food Lover's Companion* (Barron's, 2007); WebMd (webmd.com); The National Onion Association (onions-usa.org)

RED CABBAGE/CABBAGE
The New Food Lover's Companion (Barron's, 2007); *The Visual Food Lover's Guide* (Wiley, 2009); The George Mateljan Foundation (whfoods.com); USDA National Nutrient Database

PLUMS
California Dried Plums Board (californiadriedplums.org); *The New Food Lover's Companion* (Barron's, 2007); USDA National Nutrient Database

GRAPES
The California Table Grape Commission (freshcaliforniagrapes.com); *The New Food Lover's Companion* (Barron's, 2007)

EGGPLANT
Noda, Y., et al., "Antioxidant activity of nasunin, an anthocyanin in eggplant peels," *Toxicology.* 148 (2000): 119–123; *The New Food Lover's Companion* (Barron's, 2007); The Visual Food Lover's Guide (Wiley, 2009); USDA National Nutrient Database

BLACKS & TANS

OATS
The New Food Lover's Companion (Barron's, 2007); *The Visual Food Lover's Guide* (Wiley, 2009); The Whole Grains Council (wholegrainscouncil.org)

CHIA SEEDS
Navita's Naturals (navitasnaturals.com)

HEMP SEEDS
Manitoba Harvest Hemp Foods (manitobaharvest.com)

BARLEY
The Whole Grains Council (wholegrainscouncil.org)

BLACK RICE
Lotus Foods (lotusfoods.com); The Whole Grains Council (wholegrainscouncil.org)

BLACK BEANS
The George Mateljan Foundation (whfoods.com); *The New Food Lover's Companion* (Barron's, 2007); USDA National Nutrient Database; Utah State University Cooperative Extension (extension.usu.edu)

MUSHROOMS
The Mushroom Council (mushroominfo.com)

FREEKEH
Greenwheat Freekeh (greenwheatfreekeh.com.au); The Whole Grains Council (wholegrainscouncil.org)

FLAX SEEDS
The New Food Lover's Companion (Barron's, 2007); The Flax Council of Canada (flaxcouncil.ca); WebMD (webmd.com)

OLIVES
The California Olive Committee (calolive.org); Chowhound (chowhound.com); *The New Food Lover's Companion* (Barron's, 2007); USDA National Nutrient Database

QUINOA
USDA National Nutrient Database; The Whole Grains Council (wholegrainscouncil.org)

SESAME SEEDS
The New Food Lover's Companion (Barron's, 2007); *The Visual Food Lover's Guide* (Wiley, 2009)

COCONUT
The New Food Lover's Companion (Barron's, 2007); *The Visual Food Lover's Guide* (Wiley, 2009)

CHOCOLATE
Food Network (foodnetwork.com); National Confectioners' Association's Chocolate Council (thestoryofchocolate.com); *The New Food Lover's Companion* (Barron's, 2007)

RESOURCES

INDEX